Money: Two Philosophies

Two Philosophies of Money

THE CONFLICT OF
TRUST AND AUTHORITY

S. HERBERT FRANKEL

St. Martin's Press /New York

Library of Congress Catalog Card Number 77–9211

First published in the United States of America in 1978

Library of Congress Cataloging in Publication Data

Frankel, Sally Herbert, 1903–
  Two philosophies of money.

  1. Money. 2. Money—Psychological aspects.
I. Title.
HG221.F837   332.4′01   77–9211
ISBN 0–312–82698–2

Printed in Great Britain

TO MY WIFE

Contents

Preface

This book deals with the changes which have taken place in the attitude to the economic and social role of money in the free world. The present ambivalence towards the money economy rests on the ascription to money of abstract powers which it does not possess. Consequently much of what goes under the name of monetary policy arises from false or misleading analogies and from the belief that it is possible to ignore individual and social custom and convention.

It may be helpful to the reader if I set out briefly how this book deals with these issues.

In the Introduction I discuss why monetary questions are basically philosophical or moral. Chapters I and II show the significance of the cultural attitudes towards and symbolism of money as expressed particularly in the conflicting social philosophies of Karl Marx, Georg Simmel and J. M. Keynes. By contrast Chapter III discusses the actual foundations of trust and certainty in monetary policy and practice in the nineteenth century. In the course of this analysis I examine the views of Carl Menger, Macleod, Bagehot and others. The nature and relevance of the reaction against the nineteenth-century heritage is considered in Chapter IV. It emphasizes the importance of Georg Friedrich Knapp's influence on Keynes's outlook. This leads naturally to a detailed exposition in Chapter V of the Keynesian and post-Keynesian morality of money – and its assault on the monetary economy itself. Chapter VI assesses the implications of these modern ideologies for the survival of a free society.

Throughout the writing of this book I have been greatly encouraged and stimulated by the friendship of many colleagues while I was a Visiting Professor at the University of Virginia, in particular by the following, to whom I owe a debt of gratitude difficult to repay:

to Professor G. Warren Nutter who read and commented on the manuscript. As Director of The Thomas Jefferson Center for Political Economy he made arrangements which, through the generous support of the Earhart Foundation, enabled me to complete the book; to Professor William Breit who painstakingly read all the drafts of the book and made many valuable and original suggestions; to Professor John Hampton Moore for reading and commenting on the manuscript; and to Professor Peter Laughlin Heath for reading the final draft of the book and for most helpful advice on the philosophical aspects.

None of these is responsible for the views I have expressed.

Finally, I owe a special debt of gratitude to my wife for typing and editing all the versions of the book and for encouraging me to persevere with it.

I also wish to thank the Librarian of Nuffield College, Miss Christine Kennedy, and her staff, for invaluable help at all times.

Nuffield College   S.H.F.
Oxford

Introduction

. . . Men cannot enjoy the rights of an uncivil and of a civil state together.
Edmund Burke.[1]

There has been a striking development in statistical and econo-
metric analysis of monetary data, and in the clarification of logical
concepts in the theory of monetary economics in the last fifty years.
It has, however, obscured the fact that there are basic monetary
questions which are not "scientific" or "technical" but depend on
the particular vision of what men and women hold to be the truths,
principles, or values which do, or should, govern them. The
philosophy of money consists of an analysis of such questions. It
forms the subject-matter of this study.

My interest in it grew out of consideration of the differences in the
range of activities to which highly abstract concepts of calculation or
money can be meaningfully applied as between different societies,
or even within the same society.

The difficulty – I suggested many years ago[2] – arises not only
because of different technical systems of organizing production as,
for example, in market-oriented as compared with non-exchange
economies. It has its origin in the different objectives and ideals
which consciously or unconsciously dominate them.

I pointed out that the attempt by an individual to obtain income is
not merely an isolated activity, arising out of some abstract concept
of individual values, but is of a piece with social communication.
Even Robinson Crusoe did not act merely according to the dictates
of his natural appetites: he brought with him, from the society to
which he belonged, not only a stock of goods but a set of values. Our
actions are not determined in isolation: they depend also on the
influence we can exert upon others and which their activities in turn
exert upon us. Just as economic production depends on social

co-operation, so the symbolism according to which it is regulated is socially determined. "In a community of absolute pagans," I wrote, "he that wishes to build a temple to the deity would be engaged upon a social act of persuasion."[3] He could not obtain permission to embark upon such an enterprise unless his views and wishes had gained sufficient social acceptance.

When, some years ago, I mentioned to an economist that I was attempting to write a book on the philosophy of money he gave me that pitying stare of incomprehension peculiar to those who believe they have been privileged to deal in scientific certainties which others cannot but also perceive. But, as Sir Isaiah Berlin has reminded us, "one of the surest hallmarks of a philosophical question . . . is that there is no automatic technique, no universally recognised expertise, for dealing with such questions. . . . They do not . . . satisfy conditions required by an independent science, the principal among which is that the path to their solution must be implicit in their very formulation. . . . Once we do feel quite clear about how we should proceed, the questions no longer seem philosophical." He pointed out that only where the concepts are firm, clear, and generally accepted, is it possible to construct a science, formal or empirical. But " . . . where we find frequent recrimination about what can or what cannot claim to be a law, an established hypothesis, an undisputed truth . . . we are at best in the realm of quasi-science. . . . We find ourselves in the large, rich and central but unstable, volcanic and misty regions of 'ideologies'."[4]

The definitions, or descriptions, that have been applied to money are legion. They range from those which carry the implication that it is the root of all evil to those that regard it as manna from heaven. Some have argued that it does not matter, others that it matters too much. Money has been described as a political, or sociological, phenomenon, as a mechanism, as a mirror, as a religion, as a myth, as a means of communication which reduces complexity and as a distortion which increases it, as the curse of the miser and the elixir of the spendthrift, as a means to all ends and as an end in itself, as barren and as all-powerful, as inert or neutral and as "the drink which stimulates the economic system to activity", as the tool of social progress and as an obstacle to it.

Such definitions, descriptions, implications, or epithets always imply or involve a moral or philosophical issue. This is not generally recognized because Cartesian forms of thought still dominate our thinking. But, as Henry Simons wrote forty years ago, "we cannot get along . . . without some moral sanctions and mandates which politicians must obey in matters of finance".[5] But we are little further in discovering how they can be brought to do so, or in agreeing on the moral principles involved.

John Maynard Keynes was one of the few economists in this century who recognized the far-reaching importance of the connection between considerations of morality and justice – to which he frequently referred – and the monetary order.

No one has so vividly portrayed or reflected the reason and unreason in the monetary debates of his time and the irreconcilable drives and dissatisfactions of Western Society. Towards the end of his life, in completing his classic work, he added to it what he called "Concluding Notes on the Social Philosophy Towards Which the General Theory Might Lead". These concluding notes, however, as a careful reader will find, portray very much the same philosophical outlook with which, as a young man, he began. Already then he was ambivalent as between the different ways in which the contents of his moral prescriptions should be made up. This ambivalence is the consequence of what I would call the search for scientific certainty in the monetary order and for technical, mechanistic, or automatic means of controlling human behaviour in regard to it. As Henry Simons perceived, it rests on the fear of money itself. It is that fear which grips all the protagonists in the current monetary debate, and has caused philosophical issues of considerable importance to be obscured.

John Stuart Mill, in his *Principles of Political Economy with some of their Applications to Social Philosophy*, was at pains to suggest that money is of little importance relative to the more basic matters with which he was concerned. Keynes – a century later – sees money as distorting everything and wants the authority of the State to force money to reflect a less disturbing image.

It is significant however that many of the critics of Keynes and the Keynesians are themselves still enmeshed in the attempt to control the monetary order by allegedly "scientific" or technical means. Henry Simons, fearful of the State's monetary threat to liberty, appealed for a system of rules instead of authorities in order to parry it. Yet, at the moment of writing, he conceded that, owing to the exceptional conditions then prevailing, it still remained necessary to be reconciled to pure management in the money field and to rely on government action and on political efforts.[6] Conditions have apparently continued to be "exceptional" ever since he wrote. Even his most distinguished disciples have not been able to gain acceptance of any such set of agreed rules.

The attempt to make the uncertain certain is reflected in the ongoing highly sophisticated debate about the scope, legitimacy and effectiveness of monetary policy. On the one hand, there are the optimists who believe that we now possess the technical tools and scientific knowledge to enable us to control monetary behaviour, not only within a nation but even internationally, and, thereby, not only the rate of economic change, but progress also. On the other hand, their opponents would support Milton Friedman's view that:

We are in danger of assigning to monetary policy a larger role than it can perform, in danger of asking it to accomplish tasks that it cannot achieve and, as a result, in danger of preventing it from making the contribution that it is capable of making.[7]

I argue in this book that there is a far deeper issue: one which rests on that very powerful stream of thought and feeling which forms the sombre back-drop to such scintillating academic debates. Keynes, with his almost uncanny awareness of the social drives and undercurrents of his and our times, perceived it, helped to formulate it, and, finally, failed in his attempt to show how to harness it.

It arises from the belief that a free monetary order is irrelevant and has now become an anachronism, a relic of the past, and an impediment to the allegedly more "rational" policies of the present: the free monetary order should be abolished wherever it has not already been abolished, or has not already abolished itself.

A free monetary order basically implies the possibility for individuals of choosing between a multiplicity of conflicting goals or ends. It postulates the existence of principles, enforced by custom, convention and law, which ensure that its operation will not be arbitrarily, capriciously, or lightly altered in favour of particular groups, individuals, or interests. It implies therefore, as A. I. Melden has so happily formulated it, "the maintenance of the moral structure of the relations between all of the parties concerned".[8]

What, in relation to the monetary order, brings such a moral structure about? What is its relevance? What maintains it? What destroys it?

It is to such questions that Georg Simmel, the social philosopher and pioneer of modern sociology, addressed himself in his classic book *Die Philosophie des Geldes*,[9] which was first published in 1900.

It was John Maynard Keynes who made the revolt against the predominant nineteenth century view of money respectable. It was Georg Simmel, at the turn of the century, who laid bare its origins and foresaw its consequences. In these we are now entangled. Simmel did not develop any particular abstract philosophical system. His is a personal interpretation. He examined the far-reaching forces making for change in the established social and intellectual order. They are similar to ours. That is why much of his thinking, although embedded in philosophical disputes which no longer interest us, are still so relevant.

Simmel was always trying to find, in a single appearance or instance of life, the meaning of the whole. As such an instance he selected money. He related it to the political, economic, and aesthetic movements of his time – and of history.

He saw money in relativistic terms as the functional category of modern civilization: the symbol of its spirit, forms, and thought. In his analysis of the reciprocal influence of money on social attitudes and expectations he was not concerned with monetary *policy*; nor did he advocate any specific social goal. His basic interest was the freedom of the individual, the inviolability of his personality, and the effect of the money economy thereon.

Simmel did not view the institution of money in mechanical terms but rather as a conflict between our abstract conception of money and the social trust on which it rests. He was concerned to elucidate the moral basis of monetary order in contrast to the subversion of morals through money, in the abstract, which he feared.

In this study I attempt to show not only how Simmel's *Philosophy of Money* is related to the thought underlying that of the classical economists and their successors but also why it highlights the present monetary dilemma of the free world. It deals with many of the same problems as now face us and, in particular, whether a free monetary order is likely to survive. If not, to what will its disappearance be due? Is it threatened because men and women take it too much for granted; expect too much from it, misunderstand it, believe themselves thwarted or alienated by it, or simply cannot bear the burden of it? And what will be the effects of its demise?

Simmel was not only concerned by what money had done or could do *for* people but what it had done, and might do, *to* them. In Simmel's dialectic we are always in danger of being slain by those objects of our own creation which have lost their original human coefficient.[10] He was pessimistic about the likely survival of the free monetary order. In spite of the benefits conferred on civilization by it – which he analysed with profound insight – he foresaw the threats to it which could bring about its decline.

John Maynard Keynes also questioned the likelihood of the survival of the free monetary order – but for very different reasons. He most feared that it might not prove possible to make it work in terms of the specific goals which society should, in his opinion, pursue. This outlook was as different from that of Simmel, and that of the classical economists, as chalk from cheese. Freud also, it will be remembered, was pessimistic about the possibility of reconciling within civilization the discontents it generates. However, neither Simmel nor Freud were utopianists who contemplated overall experimental measures, such as might in the last resort endanger – and indeed destroy – freedom itself. Yet many of the utopianist monetary practitioners of our time have no hesitation in furthering such measures and in quoting Keynes, among others, as authority for doing so. Unfortunately, as Sir Karl Popper has pointed out, problems connected with the uncertainty of the human factor must force the utopianist to try to control it, not only by the transformation of society, according to plan, but also by the transformation of man.[11]

If this book, by contrasting two basic philosophies of money, sets them up as opposite poles, around which I also examine the views of others in this highly complex and long drawn out debate, it is unavoidable that at times I may appear to over-simplify the issues at stake. I must apologise to the reader for using this didactic device. My aim is to draw attention to the fact that we may still be debating these issues in terms of categories of thought that are no longer suitable for an elucidation of the changes in monetary form and content that now confront us.

CHAPTER I
The Symbolism of Money

"The use of money . . . gives society the technical machinery of exchange [and] the opportunity to combine personal freedom with orderly co-operation on a grand scale." Wesley C. Mitchell.[1]

Money and the Modern Spirit

An early reviewer of Georg Simmel's *The Philosophy of Money* wrote: ". . . the author looks down upon the market-place of life, the comings and goings of which seem so intricate, where people seem to be jumbled up, and where you look in vain for the *archimedean point* from which the earth can be moved out of its poles. . . ."[2] For the Victorians[3] money was that point. The certainty of the monetary order not only symbolized, but also appeared to guarantee, the beneficence of the rapidly developing free exchange economy. This is what most enraged the critics of its political and philosophical ideas – and not least those which governed the accepted role of money. It is against such ideas that the twentieth century has, as I shall show, come to revolt.

As a result it is indeed sometimes difficult for us today to recall that Wesley C. Mitchell could, during the First World War, hail the development of money as one of the great institutional advances of mankind. He found in it the basis of economic rationality. Money directed our attention away from a subjective to an objective realm of thought. He judged the case of money to be one of the great rationalizing habits slowly evolved by society and painfully learned by the individual. It gave society the basis of that abstract system of thought, and of accounting, which, following Sombart, he called "economic rationalism". . . .[4] Yet Mitchell did not, after all, escape from what I regard as the fatal ambivalence of our time: the propensity its regard money as something rather suspect, apart from, and outside, the process of social life as a whole. Thus for Mitchell, as for so many others, the making of goods and the making of money seemed to be separate processes: "at some points quite distinct from, or even opposed to each other; at most points running side by side . . ."[5]

Simmel saw the likelihood of these developments more clearly than anyone else. He laid bare the psychological reasons for them. He was, he said, exploring the conflict between order and life, indeed of "more-than-life."[6] That is why he was fascinated by the very idea of money. To him money *symbolizes* a certain form or structure but not a static one: the significance and meaning of money lie in its mobility. Even the influence which it exerts when it rests consists only in the anticipation of the renewal of it. It is a bearer of movement from which everything else has been excluded. But, it should be noted, that he also regards money as a symbol for the opposite way of making the world intelligible. It is a symbol of persistence as well as a symbol of movement. Like a universal law, it is "beyond all the movements of which it is the form and basis."[7] For Simmel, money therefore is

more than a standard of value and a means of exchange. It has a meaning and significance over and above its purely economic function. Modern society is a monetary society not merely because its economic transactions are based on money, or because its manifold aspects are influenced by money, but because it is in money that the modern spirit finds its most perfect expression.[8]

What makes his work retain its importance is that his philosophical analysis of money was not undertaken to defend an established monetary order but to examine critically the ideas and spirit which it reflects. This inescapably involved the problem of individuality and freedom.

Social Evaluations

Already in the Preface to the first edition Simmel made this quite clear. He argued that economic forms are themselves the consequence of deeper social *evaluations* and forces whose psychological, indeed, even metaphysical, assumptions must be recognized. He was concerned to transcend a purely "economic"[9] explanation of events.

As a distinguished contemporary of Simmel wrote: "The actual purpose of this book is – one could say – to determine what the money economy – especially that of the nineteenth century – has made out of Man and Society and especially of its inter-relations and institutions".[10]

I know of no work in social philosophy which throws more light on the nineteenth century ideology of money. It has been much neglected by economists but sociologists have not made this mistake. As Hugh Dalziel Duncan has recently written:

Those who attempt creation of sociological models without reading Simmel delude themselves. As many of us have discovered . . . the figure of Simmel often appears toward the end of the journey. We greet him with dismay as well as respect, for he is coming back from a point . . . we are still struggling to reach.[11]

Historical Materialism

Simmel, at the very outset,[12] emphasized that he wished to refute the basic doctrine of historical materialism, i.e. the insistence on explaining social change only in terms of extraneous economic or material causes. If it were really true that the growth of custom, law, religion, and so forth, was the result of economic development, without also fundamentally affecting it, then it was not clear what accounted for changes in economic development itself. The economic factor should be regarded as only *primus inter pares*. Marx, he argued, attempted to separate the variable from the constant factors, as if history were made up only of the former. Historical materialism was not content with the humble role of hypothetical analysis. It aspired to portray reality itself. In this it resembled the naturalistic school of painting which wanted to be exactly true to nature. Yet both are willy-nilly making a subjective selection, of what they take to be the facts of reality, in their attempt to reproduce or re-create it. Simmel thought that the success of historical materialism in gaining adherents rested less on philosophical considerations than on personal psychological motives. It was in order to incorporate the tendency towards socialism that its economic contents loomed so large. In concentrating on an appeal to the masses, it necessarily had to put economic interests to the forefront: no others could appeal with equal cer- tainty to everyone. A broadly based politico-ethical aim – unless it was a religious one – had to be based on material interests. Only these were common to all epochs of history.

But there was another reason for the connection between philo- sophical materialism and Marxism. It lay in the striving for equality. The principle of egalitarianism – and the levelling it involved – could also, for all practical purposes, be envisaged only in the economic field. For this reason also, practical socialism tended to adopt a materialistic view of life; notwithstanding that in its deeper meaning it was concerned with much more. Thus Simmel recognized historical materialism as a method of analysis and as a heuristic model of social change, in terms only of extraneous material factors.

He regarded all such attempts as based on a fundamental cate- gory mistake – a mistake which, I intend to show, also underlies much of current monetary theory and policy. It consists in regarding society as some extraneous, unique entity which has to be in exis- tence in order that all the particular interrelations of its members, such as their rank, order, cohesion, division of labour, exchange and religious community, can come into existence within its framework. This is not so. It is the interrelations themselves that go to make up society, which is identical with them, and is constituted by them. Society is nothing but the combined expression, the general name, for the totality of such interrelations. It is not something additional to or, as it were, an extra member standing outside them.[13]

A Category Mistake

Simmel is here referring to that type of category mistake which, as Professor Ryle has explained, arises from representing facts "as if they belonged to one logical type or category . . . when they actually belong to another". He gives the following example:

A foreigner visiting Oxford or Cambridge for the first time is shown a number of colleges, libraries, playing fields, museums, scientific depart- ments and administrative offices. He then asks "But where is the Univer- sity? I have seen where the members of the Colleges live, where the Registrar works, where the scientists experiment and the rest. But I have not yet seen the University in which preside and work the members of your University." It has then to be explained to him that the University is not another collateral institution, some ulterior counterpart to the colleges, laboratories and offices which he has seen. The University is just the way in which all that he has already seen is organized. When they are seen and when their co-ordination is understood, the University has been seen. His mistake lay in his innocent assumption that it was correct to speak of Christ Church, the Bodleian Library, the Ashmolean Museum, *and* the University, to speak that is as if "the University" stood for an extra member of the class of which these other units are members. He was mistakenly allocating the University to the same category as that to which the other institutions belong.[14]

Similarly, money appears to be something additional to, or to stand outside, the individual things themselves, as if it were "an empire of its own". This is, writes Simmel, an illusion: not things but people are responsible for the activities involved.

He illustrates the same category mistake in the misuse of concepts like wealth, capital, and property, when they are thought of as existing apart from or outside the socially determined rights which they express, or the exercise thereof which they permit. The expression of these rights in money terms is particularly prone to give rise to this error. Money is nothing outside the objects, services or rights to which it gives access. What we really have in mind, when we speak of the characteristic power of money, are the wider unspecified uses which it commands, as compared with those which can be obtained by the possession of any particular commodity or right. Money has, or appears to have, that unique potential power of being incorporated in any future use that its possessor may desire to put it to. Yet, in fact, even this power and potentiality is not one which stands outside, or is additional to, those eventual uses. If they are no longer available, or permitted, the apparent independent power of money disappears with them.

Money and Exchange

Simmel makes the same point in regard to the process of exchange: outside it "money is as little as regiments and flags without collective aggression and defence, or priests and temples without a common religion". The function of exchange is one of the purest and pristine forms of socialization. Acts of exchange are not the *consequence of the pre-existence of a perfected society*. Exchange comes about through the proximity of individuals in some form of inter-relationship. Money is not a consciously created artifact, but grows out of, reflects, and in turn affects the ever-changing relationships between individuals and the society which they compose. That is why the creation of values through exchange is as important to Simmel as it is anathema to Marx and his successors: In the world of reality our ego is nothing but an atom; in the world of values we are masters and creators. Nature does not care for what we care for; she destroys what seemed to be made for eternity and conserves what seems doomed to destruction but no such determinism regulates the relation between reality and value.

The fact that money grew out of the process of exchange is of prime importance because it involves the freedom of individual valuation – without which money cannot function fully as money. Whenever freedom of expressing values in money is abrogated the function of money is correspondingly curtailed. Without this freedom money loses its *raison d'être* as the medium for expressing, incorporating and symbolizing the contractual relationships between individuals: whether made in the past, the present or extending into the future. There is an intimate relationship between money and freedom; between the keeping of promises and the certainty of contracts; between social function and the rule of law. None of these relations is regarded by Simmel as a mere link in a chain of mechanical interactions: for him money is in the last resort an abstract form. Moreover, since form and content are relative terms, "every new content enables him to raise the level of abstraction, and the higher the level of abstraction the richer the variety of contents *suggested* by the form."[15] In this tendency to increasing abstraction lies the clue to Simmel's view as to the origin of some of the most troublesome aspects of the nineteenth century conception of the role of money. Forms survive the conditions that produce them, whether in the field of money, religion, law, culture or art. This autonomy permits them to endure even after the conditions have changed. Similarly money, as it develops ever more sophisticated forms, finally comes to be regarded as incorporating the purest form of potentiality – of potential power itself. What so impressed Simmel was that money developed far beyond its purely technical or mechanized function as a medium of exchange. The modern competitive economy had brought its function as a store-of-value to the highest possible degree of abstraction. Therefore it came to be regarded as the most certain, and most powerful, means of attaining not only known or immediate ends chosen by the individual but also the most remote: even the as yet unformulated desires which he might conceive.

One of the basic facts of our subjective world was that we express social relations through symbolic images. Money was one of these. From being a functional it had become a symbolic expression of economic relationships.[16] But Simmel warned – and it is a warning of importance today – that such symbolic images could not be divorced from the circumstances which gave rise to them and to which they were bound.

To the Greeks money appeared to be little other than a necessary evil. This was because their economic efforts were directed mainly to providing goods for relatively immediate consumption based on agricultural production, and on the security that ownership of land provided. The continuity of life was thus symbolized in terms of the fixity and permanence of its contents.

In the modern world, Simmel argued, the symbolic image which money reflects was the very antithesis of that conception. It portrayed unity and interdependence not in substance but in the constant interplay of dynamic abstract forces and social relations. For example, the measuring function of money was no longer linked to a visible, tactile, transportable commodity. It was no longer merely a means of equating the values of particular things. It was conceived of as the abstract expression of values in general: divorced from the material forms in which they were incorporated.

The contrast has been strikingly described as follows:[17]

Central to Simmel's presentation of the problem of individuality is his analysis of the contrast between the philosophical outlook of the eighteenth century and that of the nineteenth.

The Enlightenment sought to emancipate man from the historical bonds of traditional institutions. In liberating men from servitude to the past, it believed it was liberating a human nature that was common to all, identical in each human being. Human freedom could be achieved simply by releasing men from the conditions which cause inequality. In this sense, the eighteenth century stood for a break with one's predecessors.

Individualism in the nineteenth century, on the other hand, meant a break with one's contemporaries. Especially under the impetus of the romantic movement, men were stimulated to differentiate themselves. Individuals had to be liberated from custom and convention so as to be most truly themselves. Freedom was thought to be the consequence of encouraging men to be infinitely differentiated and diversified, even if this entailed drastic inequalities. In short, Simmel remarks, "Eighteenth-century liberalism put the individual on his own feet: in the nineteenth, he was allowed to go as far as they would carry him."[18]

For Simmel it is a negative aspect of money that it places us at a widening distance from the objects of our own concern. Thus immediacy of impression of things and of our interests becomes weakened. Our contact with them becomes interrupted: we sense them only through the mediation of money which however can never fully express their unique and genuine character. But for that very reason money is also the solvent of personal and social bonds. It had been the liberalizing agent in medieval society: the serf was freed from his master, and the individual from the constraint of non-monetary obligations to others. This progressive emancipation of the individual from feudal and sometimes even from national ties appeared to him, and to many of his contemporaries, to be the most paramount and beneficent aspect of the free monetary order.

Ideology of Money

In my opinion, this view illustrates the change which has since taken place in attitudes to, or what might be called the "moral ideology" of money. It is surely significant that currently – even in the free world – the notion that people are entitled to use money as they please, is regarded with considerable scepticism. This completely overlooks the fact, to which Simmel referred frequently, that money contributes to the extension of individual personality and facilitates the development of an ever widening circle of economic interdependence based on the dispersion of trust. Under conditions of direct barter trust is confined to the parties immediately involved. The use of money extends it to the people of the village, of the tribe, of the nation, and finally, to vast areas of the world. Highly inventive and sophisticated monetary transactions enable diverse operations to take place in insurance, banking, commodity trading, foreign exchange and investment, which suit the special needs of risk-bearers and risk-takers around the globe. Such transactions,

however, appear abstract, intellectual, sophisticated, out and separate from social reality. Consequently they give rise to misunderstanding and resentment. Their complexity arouses suspicion, hos-
tility and, finally, fear of the apparently mystical money itself.
Demands arise for the abolition or curtailment of what appears to
be but barren speculation. Such demands arise from a nostalgic
yearning for the seemingly natural, visible, concrete and comforting
age of barter. It is often reflected in the belief in visible government
economic controls or action.

There is nothing new in such suspicion of money transactions. In
the sixteenth century, writes Fernand Braudel,[19] most contemporaries found money "a difficult cabbala to understand" and the
increasing use of credit instruments, such as the bill of exchange,
even more so. Few could grasp their meaning or how they worked.
That credit is simply the exchange of two deferred *promises*: "I will
do something for you, you will pay me later" is even today often
obscured by obfuscating jargon which gives rise to amazement. The
scandal arising out of the activities of the Italian merchant, who
settled in Lyons about 1555, with only a table and an ink-stand, and
who made a fortune out of pledging his word on bills of exchange,
would hardly appear unjustified to many today.

The fear of money lies at the root of many of our present perplexities. For the nineteenth century, however, it was not fear of money
that predominated – it was faith in it: particularly faith in its power
to ensure certainty for the individual. Therefore nothing should be
permitted to undermine the certainty of money itself.

Simmel had no illusion as to what enabled money to play this all
pervading role. It was the freedom and security of the economic
order on which the full potentiality of money rested.[20] He did not, as
we have noted, view that potential only in historical, quantitative,
mechanical, or even functional terms. By the full potential of money
he meant the manner in which money affected not only our actions
but the fears, hopes and desires on which they were based. The mere
presence or absence, availability or scarcity, of money could acti-
vate or inhibit them. The extension of credit could itself be regarded
as a dual – indeed an uncanny – process: what was a mere future
claim, or indeed possibly only an ephemeral hope, in the hand of the
lender, appeared at the very same time as something real in the
hand of the debtor, for whom it was immediately available and
expendable. The intellectual abstractions and expectations which

made this duality possible depended entirely on the social order: on a particular conception and reality of mutual personal and social interrelations.

It is because money is a sociological phenomenon, a form of social interaction among people, that its true nature emerges ever more clearly the more intimate and dependable social bonds become. That paper money could become the instrument of the highest monetary function, and even be used as a store of value, was possible only in social groups closely knit by mutual guarantees for protection from external and especially also from internal dangers. Money was, for Simmel, a hidden force incorporating and giving rise to powerful psychological drives and expectations. It was nothing less than the immovable Mover ("der unbewegte Beweger") himself. Whilst, taken singly in the practical world it is the most transient of things in its ideal sense it is the measure of everything – the most constant of all.

It could be asked whether such a view should not be regarded as unduly extravagant. That would be to miss the point of Simmel's analysis. He was concerned with the hidden dichotomy within the money economies of Europe and beyond which the growing prosperity during the nineteenth century had obscured. It was taken for granted that the monetary trust on which it had been built would continue. Simmel was not sure that it would. There were destructive, irrational forces at work which were, to Europe's peril, generally and dangerously ignored.

CHAPTER II

Money and Individuality

The deepest problems of modern life derive from the claim of the individual to preserve the autonomy and individuality of his existence in the face of overwhelming social forces, of historical heritage, of external culture, and of the technique of life. The fight with nature which primitive man has to wage for his *bodily* existence attains in this modern form its latest transformation. Georg Simmel.[1]

The Legacy of the Eighteenth Century

No greater contrast can be imagined than that which separates many of our current conceptions of the nature and purpose of money from those which were dominant for most of the nineteenth century. To understand the latter one must appreciate the reverberations caused by the monetary disasters of the eighteenth century.

On the eve of the French Revolution there was a storm of disapproval of the Government throughout France. It concerned the creation of a new interest-bearing paper money which the king's edict had proclaimed. The edict had to be withdrawn. The Parlement in a session of 30 January 1789 expressed the fear that the New money might be appropriated by the Treasury for its own use. One parish argued: "above all we will not countenance the introduction of a paper money or a national bank, either of which can only produce a great evil, and of which the memories alone are capable of frightening us. . . ."[2] They had in mind the disastrous currency experiments of John Law, who had died sixty years before. However, their memories did not save the franc of the Revolution from a second colossal currency debacle – the rise and fall of the Assignat.[3] John Law had been inspired by the palatable belief that an abundance of money is the royal road to wealth. After the currency debacle there had been a tremendous reaction to his views throughout Europe. All and sundry now vied in again insisting that money far from being all powerful, as Law had maintained, was really nothing.[4]

It is worth reminding ourselves that Law defined money simply as an instrument of circulation, and ignored its function as a store of value. He regarded hoarding of money as an *offence* on the part of the citizens: therefore the Government had the right to take charge of the money reserves of individuals. He contrasted the costliness of the precious metals with the cheapness of paper money. With prophetic insight he remarked that whereas the majority of men say "that the credit of a particular note is based on, and is maintained by, *the freedom to accept or reject it*;" he believed "that the credit of this note is in doubt and its circulation limited, precisely because its acceptance is left *free*. The first man to reject the note . . . spreads the fear that the issuer of the note, . . . will not be in a position to supply the sum marked on the note; . . . On the other hand, if everybody *were compelled to accept the note, it might never be returned at all, and the issuer would never be compelled to redeem it*".[5]

It is therefore not surprising that by the middle of the nineteenth century discrediting of these ideas had gone so far that John Stuart Mill could, without appearing to be expressing an unusual notion, write: "There cannot, in short be intrinsically a more insignificant thing in the economy of society than money; except in the character of a contrivance for sparing time and labour. It is a machine for doing quickly and commodiously, what would be done, though less quickly and commodiously, without it, and like many other kinds of machinery, *it only exerts a distinct and independent influence of its own when it gets out of order*."[6] The issue which remained unexplained in this oft-quoted passage was what getting out of order meant; and whether the mechanical analogy did not confuse its elucidation. What, in particular, I wish to stress is that it would have seemed absurd to Mill, writing as a social philosopher, and also to the classical economists in general, that society could be improved by altering the basic function, or reducing the importance, of money itself.[7]

Challenge to Monetary Order

The difference between the accepted attitude which prevailed in the nineteenth century and that which has developed since the First World War, and particularly since the nineteen thirties, lies elsewhere: in that the very idea of the beneficence of a free monetary order was again challenged. The challenge was not only to the idea that money is "neutral". It went further. It raised the issue whether an economy based on a free monetary order was necessarily more desirable than a non-monetary economy. Thus Keynes, for example, frequently referred to the advantages of the latter and the evils of the former. He resuscitated many of the ideas of critics of the established monetary order. He eulogized men like Silvio Gesell, J. A. Hobson and A. F. Mummery, who previously had been regarded as monetary cranks like John Law. They had not only criticized the functioning of the monetary order but in their views on savings had revolted, like Karl Marx, against the optimistic assertion "that the effective love of money", which caused the savings to be made, is "the root of all economic good".[8]

Disapproval of money itself was, of course, nothing new. It goes back to antiquity. What was now made fashionable by Keynes was the formal rejection of the monetary orthodoxy of the nineteenth century. As a result the issues involved were once again discussed in more fundamental terms – as they had not been since Karl Marx.

To Marx, "Money abuses all the Gods of mankind and changes them into commodities. It has, therefore, deprived the whole world, both the human world and nature, of their own proper value. Money is the alienated essence of man's work and existence, this essence dominates him and he worships it."[9]

As opposed to the predominantly optimistic view of the Victorians, for Marx money cannot be regarded as a means to freedom:

money and religion, both products of alienated man, tyrannized over man and live lives of their own . . . under the sway of egoistic need he can only affirm himself and produce objects in practice by subordinating his products and his own activity to the domination of an alien entity and by attributing to them the significance of an alien entity, namely money.[10]

Historically the growth of exchange value and of the power of money are interconnected, and the whole exchange relationship "establishes itself as a force externally opposed to the producers and independent of them".[11]

In *The Communist Manifesto* Marx and Engels say of the bourgeoisie that they have "resolved personal work into exchange value", and have "reduced the family relation to a mere money relation". Some twenty years later, in the first volume of *Capital*, Marx speaks of money as the radical leveller that effaces all distinctions, that is to say, all distinctions other than differences in wealth. Marx exaggerated the importance in bourgeois society of wealth as compared with forms of power and prestige which are often as harmful as wealth and as little connected with estimable qualities in their possessors.[12]

Much more important, however, is Marx's attitude to exchange as such. It lies at the root of his condemnation of money and of individual freedom within a monetary economy. Most of his writing is about production for *exchange* and *sale* on the market. This he contrasts with production for *direct use*, in which *commercial* principles do not intervene in the economic relations between men.[13]

It is hardly possible to exaggerate Marx's idealization of the organization of pre-capitalist economies producing for "direct use". These he called "Asiatic", "ancient", "feudal" and "Germanic". His view about them might have been somewhat different if he had been more closely acquainted with, or had assessed more objectively, the true nature of the primitive economic conditions which he idealized: the famines, the high rates of mortality and morbidity, and the fears and uncertainties of the individual in the countries and regions of the world where production for direct use had predominated for generations. Today we know much more about the conditions of life to which individuals in societies, with such meagre margins of economic defence against the vagaries of the environment, were condemned owing to lack of market-oriented production.

However, Marx built his utopia on an idealized conception of the economic organization in such societies.[14] According to Marx, exchange is the root cause of individuals being independent of each other, rather than directly associated as in the family or in a communal – particularly a pre-capitalist – society. Thus he sees exchange making "independent communities dependent and . . . dependent members within communities independent".[15]

Marx wrote:

But man is only individualized through the process of history. He originally appears as a generic being, a tribal being, a herd animal. . . . Exchange itself is a major agent of this individualization. It makes the herd animal super-fluous and dissolves (the herd).[16]

As we shall see later the fears of the herd animal in the search for safety in economic and monetary affairs are again much to the fore over a century after Marx.

The point which I wish to stress here is that for Marx commodity exchange and, of course, especially commodity exchange expressed in terms of money, appears as an *abstract* relationship as against the *concrete* relationships existing under earlier pre-capitalist condi-tions. Money, particularly in its abstract form, is inserted between these direct personal relations. Marx in his *Capital* says that when production is for direct use, as in feudal society: there is no necessity for labour and its products to assume a "fantastic form different from their reality" because, as services in kind and payments in kind, they assume the *natural* form of labour, and not, as in a society based on production of commodities, its general *abstract* form.

It is also to this abstract quality of exchange and money relation-ships that Marx ascribes the crisis of alienation, and in his terms, of the *loss* of freedom of the individuals within society. In his utopia there will be restored to them the natural relations of an imaginary Golden Age.

For Marx alienation is not a psychiatric phenomenon but a con-sequence of objective economic conditions embedded in the exchange and monetary economy.[17] It was precisely for this reason that he regarded the bourgeois freedom of contract as illusory. Individuals might think they were freer than before because their conditions of life seemed to them accidental. But, of course, he argued, they were really less free because they were subjected to the violence of the market and the anarchy of commodity exchange. In other words, they were no longer in the secure womb of the natural pre-monetary pre-exchange society.

Marx did not, however, analyse capitalism in terms of *individual* choices and attitudes. He did not base his criticism on shortcomings of the capitalists. "To treat the capitalist as idiosyncratic or immoral was incompatible with his view of economic evolution as a process of natural history";[18] and it was not reasonable to "make the indi-vidual responsible for relations whose creature he socially remains, however he may subjectively raise himself above them".[19] For the same reason Marx regarded the capitalist's passion for wealth as "the effect of the social mechanism, of which he is but one of the wheels . . . competition makes the immanent laws of capitalist production to be felt by each individual capitalist as external coercive laws".[20] As we shall see, this historical determinism takes on a quite different form in the case of Keynes and his successors. It becomes a mechanical device of state policy, of which the entrepreneur and the capitalist are regarded merely as puppets.

The Philosophy of Georg Simmel

At first sight Simmel's philosophical approach to money seems similar to that of Marx. This is not a mere co-incidence. Simmel's theory of culture resembles Marx's philosophy of history. Both Marx and Simmel were students of Hegel's philosophy and derived from it important elements of their own doctrines. But "for Simmel, Marx does not go far enough: there is tension between the life of the individual or society and *all* of the products created by men. The dialectic must be generalized". Weingartner[21] has called Marx's theory of the dialectic of history a "Cosmic Comedy" and, in contrast, Simmel's theory of culture a "Human Tragedy". For, "in Marx's conception, the opposition between the economic order and all others will finally be resolved in the synthesis of the classless society". But the tensions Simmel is concerned with originate "in the nature of human life and will exist as long as life exists". Weingartner goes on to ask whether, even if we grant Simmel his theory of culture, it justifies his *fin de siècle* pessimism with regard to the development of the human personality. As this century comes to a close one may well ask why this pessimism has survived so long. As I show later the thinking of Keynes was permeated by it, and his followers have not been able to escape from it. Simmel's interest in the philosophy of money rests on his view that money epitomized and illustrated his theory of culture and the tensions the latter involved for the individual. He regarded culture or cultivation[22] as a process, and he is primarily concerned with its consequences for the free development of the personality of the individual: with his unease within, dependence upon, and ambivalence towards the objective world of culture and its form, which he strives to perfect in order to perfect himself. Money is one of these institutional forms. It is important to appreciate that Simmel's conception of culture

makes central neither the objects created by men, nor the process by which these objects are created, but the process of their reassimilation. Works of art or systems of science have their genesis in the experience of men. Because of this, their origin, and because of what they are, Simmel adopts Hegel's term and calls the totality of such human products *objective spirit*. . . . Culture (or better, cultivation) designates a particular relation between the individual and objective spirit; it is a process whereby the individual interiorizes the objects he finds everywhere around him.[23]

Professor Charles Taylor has recently explained the term objective spirit by pointing out that many of our most important experiences would be impossible outside of society, as for instance the experience of participating in a rite, or of taking part in the political life of our society. They are not like facts of nature, but are partly constituted by the ideas which underlie them. The institutions and practices of a society are a kind of language:

But what is "said" in this language is not ideas which could be in the minds of certain individuals only, they are rather common to a society, because embedded . . . in practices and institutions which are of the society indivisibly. In these the spirit of the society is in a sense objectified. They are to use Hegel's term "objective spirit".[24]

But in Simmel's view the individual has to pay for cultural self-improvement by accepting the tragic chance that these objective self-sufficient worlds will develop with a logic of their own[25] which will draw them farther and farther away from him.

Simmel's emphasis, in one way or another, is always on the personality of the individual. The development of human abilities and interests can be regarded as cultural advance only when each serves to develop the individual's personality as a whole. Contrary to Marx's attitude to wealth, Simmel held the view that in general every one of man's possessions involves an extension of his being: of his subjective life. What he does with the things which are his is a function of his individuality, his will, his feelings, his mode of thinking. For primitive man objective and subjective experience remains comparatively undifferentiated.

In primitive Societies the land belongs collectively to the kin as a whole, the livestock belongs collectively to the special sub-family, but the mobile goods are the property of the individual, for they are supposed to be destroyed after his death. The most mobile of all kinds of properties is money. Consequently, there is a close interrelationship between the development of a money economy and the growth of the role of the individual and the recognition which is given to him.[26]

The same occurred in regard to the relation between the owner and his property. Money alone made possible the complete separation of the first from the second. In primeval times personal relationships were dominant. Feudal institutions modified this situation. The medieval corporation fully absorbed the individual, but the corporations remained clearly distinct and separate. Only in the modern sophisticated money economy were both property and its owners completely differentiated – and liberated – from each other.

Scientific Objectivity and Abstract Freedom

Simmel drew a parallel between the increasing scientific objectivity with which modern man conceived of the universe and his attempt to express individual freedom in similar abstract terms. The more pronounced the abstract objective concepts concerning the real order of things became, the greater was felt to be the need to express personal individuality by them also. It was an attempt to rescue the equilibrium of man's inner life.

However, all this clearly involves a cost. It is easy to picture freedom merely as independence from the will of others. This is an over-simplification. It may describe the position of the frontiersman, the backwoodsman, the solitary settler, or the Christian or Hindu hermit, because freedom originally appears as an absence of all social restraint. But for a social being freedom has a much more positive meaning. It appears as a continuous process of emancipation: as a right to enter voluntarily into dependence, as a struggle which must be renewed after each victory. It is a *process* of incessant liberation from restraints which limit in reality, or attempt to limit ideally, the independence of the individual. "It is not a being, but a becoming, a sociological activity".[27]

In the complex money economy of the industrialized modern world independence is more positive in one sense and less so in another. Modern man requires the services and co-operation of innumerable others and would be quite helpless without them.

Money, it is true, connects him with them in a non-personal way and this gives him a feeling of not being beholden to them. In fact the development of civilization has made him more dependent than ever before on the objective bonds with them and on ever more objects to boot. The money economy, while enhancing freedom in one sense, in another subtly diminishes it by endeavouring to express in money, in averages, and in aggregates, personal relations and qualities – even ascetic and artistic ones. These become less diverse, less unique, less characterized by standards of excellence.

The World of Measure

Modern man is above all else a mathematician, a statistician and an accountant. His theoretical world is to be understood in terms of mathematical formulae. His practical world is to be weighed and measured in terms of quantities of pleasure and pain. His political world is to be run on the basis of counting votes.[28]

Indeed, the money economy is merely the sublimation of economic life. Money expresses the purely economic aspects of objects just as logic expresses their intellectual or conceptual ones. Money is a mirror which pictures all elements with complete indifference to non-monetary values. If it is true, Simmel suggests, that the predominant style of art influences our way of viewing nature, then the quantitative structure of monetary relations, which is superimposed upon qualitative actuality, must greatly influence our way of viewing it. The calculating intellect which operates through the money economy receives back from that same money economy some of the mental characteristics in terms of which it dominates modern life. There is an analogy between the mentality which the money economy engenders and the conviction that nothing is real in any ultimate sense if it cannot be measured. This objective and impersonal character of money, indeed its very lack of character, is important in the development of individuality. Money acts, as it were, in a double role: On the one hand it negates the subjective, the unique and the qualitative factors, on the other it allows the individual to realize his personal ends by impersonal means.[29]

Two Forms of Individualism

Simmel was concerned to make a distinction between two forms[30] of individualism. The one was that of the eighteenth century which, as with Kant, was characterized by the emphasis on freedom. The other lay in Romanticism, with its emphasis on uniqueness, as in the anti-intellectualism of thinkers like Carlyle and Nietzsche. The contrast between the philosophical outlook of the eighteenth century and that of the nineteenth is central to Simmel's treatment of individuality. In seeking to emancipate man from the historical bonds of traditional institutions, the enlightenment believed it was liberating a human nature that was common to all. Human freedom was to be achieved simply by a break with the past to release the individual from the conditions which had caused inequality. By contrast, for the nineteenth century individualism involved a break with one's contemporaries. Individuals to be most truly themselves were, under the influence of the romantic movement, stimulated to differentiate themselves from others and to liberate themselves from custom and convention. As Simmel succinctly put it, "Eighteenth-century liberalism put the individual on his own feet: in the nineteenth he was allowed to go as far as they would carry him".[31]

The fundamental attitude of the eighteenth century was, in brief, that individuals are homogeneous and basically undifferentiated. They can therefore be bound together solely by means of law which can be applied indiscriminately to one and all – since one and all are essentially alike. This is a quantitative individualism that treats the individual as a unit, as a separate entity. Simmel calls it the individualism of singleness (*Einzelheit*).

In contrast to this conception the nineteenth century developed a qualitative individualism of uniqueness (*Einzigheit*). As single, one attains the freedom that is permitted to whatever falls within the law. As unique, one is free by falling outside the law. As single, one is an instance, an exemplification, of mankind. As unique, one's context is society, which exists as the background against which one stands out: one's fellow men conveniently provide one with innumerable points of unlikeness.

The romantic feels that his self is absolutely specific and irreplaceable. Individuality becomes precious because it is incomparable; priceless because matchless. Yet one's uniqueness escapes possession. It remains an ideal to be longed for: the individual seeks his self "as if he did not yet have it".[32]

Simmel contrasted the quantitative and qualitative aspects of individualism. He regarded the first as a by-product both of intellectualism and of the money economy and the second as a spiritual reaction against it. For him, money, intellectualism and law in their institutional forms, all necessarily exemplify indifference to individual idiosyncrasy. They do not, however, for this reason represent a withdrawal from reality and its stubborn contrariness and concreteness. Rather they are the unavoidable means by which alone we can attempt to transform or regulate it. However, in doing so these institutional forms have introduced an abstract factor whose own norms are necessarily quite indifferent to, indeed only intensify, the contradictions within reality – within life itself. Simmel's prophetic explorations of the basic schisms within the money economy rest on his view of the relations between the individual, the culture of his society and the techniques of civilization.

For him money was not something extraneous to the social order. It was not, as for Marx, something which like the State would one day wither away and thus ensure man's emancipation. It was not an alien force dominating men's lives. Rather, it was a fragile constituent of the growth of personality, and of civilization itself, which could not be conceived of without it, any more than without the powers of abstract reason on which it was based. But like them the powers of abstract money could be abused, and could lead to the abuse of freedom. That is what Simmel feared most.

The Significance of Moses Hess

The difference between the views on money of Marx and Simmel is also reflected in the difference between that of Marx and Moses Hess, the main founder of early German Socialism. Hess, though despised by Marx for his idealism, influenced Marx's concept of the abstract nature of money. The differences between Hess and Marx on this question relate also to the differences between the two philosophies of money with which I am concerned in this book. I therefore end this chapter with a brief consideration of them.[33]

Hess's memorandum on money[34] was known to Marx. The similarities of thought and language with Marx's writings on alienation of the individual through money and exchange are striking. It is not possible to record them in detail here. I refer therefore only to some examples of Hess's views on this problem. He argued that in his spiritual life the individual surrendered or alienated his being to God because he wanted to obtain immortality which was unattainable without Him. So he needed God for his individual existence, for his holy immortal soul, for his salvation. For this reason Hess saw in Christianity the logic and essence of egoism, which he thought was paralleled in the practical life of the individual by the alienation of his being and activity in money. Like God, money stood over and against the individual like a foreign power which dominated and enslaved him. In this topsy-turvy world, what God represented in the individual's spiritual life money represented in his practical life: the alienated substance of mankind – the disgrace, the confusion and the confounding of its life's work.

It should be noted that, as in Marx, these views revolve around the evil of economic exchange and especially exchange in terms of money. For Hess, money is the indelible brand-mark stamped in figures on the forehead of human beings, who are, indeed, free to buy and sell themselves, yet remain nothing but slaves. Among them we must not only number the workers. Politicians and capitalists also purchase their individual existence through the loss of their freedom. All must be counted among those miserable creatures that have to devour each other: who cannot be freely creative unless they are prepared to starve.

One could quote from many other passages in this strain but what I regard as important are not the similarities with the views of Marx but the vast gulf that really separates Hess from them.

What has to be stressed is that the state of monetary corruption which Hess describes is not regarded by him as external to man – it lies within him. It is not the money as an outside force which is his corruptor. Money only reflects what individuals themselves make of society.

When it came to the crunch: to the crucial question whether or not all the monetary evils – which he had so vehemently denounced – could not be done away with, by the abolition of money, the answer that Hess gave was clear and sharp. It was that money could no more be abolished on command than it had been created on command. The need was for mankind to seek its unification not by lusting after and pursuing material and spiritual idols but by the desire to bring about a new social order resting on an inner unification of men through love. If this were done, then the material idols – and among them money – would be destroyed.

As, Sir Isaiah Berlin has noted, it turned out that Hess had a deeper understanding of some essential matters than more gifted and sophisticated thinkers.

In his socialist days – and they only ceased with his death – he said that the abolition of property and the destruction of the middle classes did not necessarily and automatically lead to paradise; for they did not necessarily cure injustice or guarantee social or individual equality. This was a bold and original view for a socialist of those days. His allies were, for the most part, men dominated by a desire for a clear-cut structure, and a rationalist, rather than rational, desire to solve social problems in almost geometrical, black and white terms. . . . In this dogmatic and intolerant *milieu* Hess permitted himself to doubt whether any solution could, in principle, achieve this, unless and until the men who built the new world themselves lived by the principles of justice, and felt benevolence and love towards individual human beings and not merely humanity at large, that is to say, were endowed with a character and an outlook which no amount of social and political reform could of itself secure.[35]

It remains to add the noteworthy fact that Hess, like so many others in the cultured Europe of his time, recognized that the egoistic, materialistic, and what they regarded as the mad competitive struggle, had resulted in much unanticipated good: it had developed the abilities and aptitudes of individuals. Hess thought that these egoistic drives could be dispensed with. The productive powers of mankind could no longer be developed further and his efforts to perfect them further were fruitless and wasted. The old social order had had its day and so too had money. Thus, whereas Marx built his Utopia on the return to primitive non-monetary forms of social organization, Hess laboured under the Utopian illusion that mankind's productive problems were already mainly solved.

One can well conclude as did Silberner[36] that, if Hess were to be resurrected, the social Welfare State of the West would hardly surprise him. He had foreseen it: since he believed that in a democratic republic all social reforms could eventually be accomplished without civil war. But he would be most distressed at the absence of the socialist society for which he lived and fought. One might add that the general development of authoritarianism would appear almost unbelievable to him.

CHAPTER III

The Nineteenth Century Ideology

Credit is a power which may grow, but cannot be constructed. Those who live under a great and firm system of credit must consider that if they break up that one they will never see another, for it will take years upon years to make a successor to it. Walter Bagehot.[1]

The Miracle of Credit

One has only to read Bagehot's classic book *Lombard Street* to experience the sense of wonderment and pride inspired, at the height of the Victorian era, by the Banker to the World – the City of London – "the greatest combination of economical power and economic delicacy that the world has ever seen".[2]

But what precisely did Bagehot mean when he wrote "money is economical power" and that England was the greatest moneyed power in the world? He was not referring to its "immediately disposable and ready cash", or liquid balances as we would now say. He was referring to the "borrowable money": the concentration of funds in the London Money Market which greatly exceeded that of all of Europe put together.[3] On this rested the miracle of new credit creation. It was this which to the Victorians appeared so remarkable, so inventive, so exciting, and so beneficial. In Lombard Street credit could always be obtained upon good security or on good prospects. Elsewhere the world languished for want of it.

Trust

A place like Lombard Street was "a luxury which no country has ever enjoyed with even comparable equality before". By this he meant that it was a heritage from the past: a result of the growth of personal character and of the reputation for reliability. In short, it rested on trust. For "credit in business is like loyalty in Government". It is true, he argued, that a theorist could easily map out a scheme of government in which Queen Victoria could be dispensed with because the House of Commons is the real sovereign; but for practical purposes, he thought, such arguments are not even worth examining. If those millions, who then loyally obeyed Queen Victoria without doubt and without reasoning, were to begin to argue it would not be easy to persuade them to obey Queen Victoria or anything else. Effectual arguments to convince the people who need convincing would be wanting.

So also with the immense system of credit founded on the Bank of England:

The English people, and foreigners too, *trust it implicitly*. Every banker knows that if he has to *prove* that he is worthy of credit, however good may be his arguments, in fact his credit is gone: *but what we have requires no proof. The whole rests on* an instinctive confidence generated by use and years.[4]

No wonder that for Simmel it was that faith and belief in the public *certainty* of the monetary order on which rested money's potential: its power of promise and performance. For him there was much more at stake here than mere confidence in the money mechanism: that the soundness of the coins of the realm would be maintained as to the prescribed weight and fineness and paper money issued in accordance with the rules laid down. Something else had to be added. Without that additional, integrating ingredient even the most superlative coin – as regards weight and fineness – could not completely fulfil its function. That additional ingredient was nothing other than the faith, belief and trust which the coin symbolizes. It was expressed by the inscription on Maltese coins which read "Non aes sed fides".

He regarded this as much more than a convenient symbol to facilitate exchange and financial transactions. It was a unique, notional and abstract guarantee by society to the holder of money that he would be able to continue to turn it to account and to dispose of it without loss. It arose because as soon as money had replaced barter a third party – society itself – had come into the picture: the fulcrum of erstwhile relationships between the two parties to the barter agreement had been shifted. Now each was no longer dependent only on his relation to the other but also on relations to the economic circle which, in an abstract and indefinable way, guaranteed the functioning and acceptability of the money they made use of. The indefinable character of this guarantee arose, of course, from the obvious fact that no one who was the possessor of money could actually force anyone to give him goods or services for it. The claim to exchange the money into goods and services was always potential. That is why there was some element of faith and trust – that is credit – in all money, even in metallic money. The latter also is always, in the last resort, a promise by society as a whole, which the act of coinage or, correspondingly, the imprint on paper money symbolizes. In this connection Simmel compares money to a bill of exchange drawn on society on which the name of the drawee has not been filled in. The guarantee which, through its rulers or representatives, society assumes is like discounting the probability that, although everyone is free to reject its money, each individual will, in fact, take it.

Custom

Why this should be so was a problem which had concerned Carl Menger long before Simmel's first article on the subject. For him the origin of money was best thought of as "the unintended result, as the unplanned outcome of specifically *individual* efforts of members of a society".[5]

Menger regarded custom as the most decisive factor in the development of money. As James Bonar later so pithily expressed it: "the dollar was made by law the currency when custom had made it so *de facto*".[6]

For Menger money was a social institution.[7] It was the result of an evolutionary process. This was as difficult to explain – and as important to understand – as the origin of law. "National law in its most original form was, ... not the result of a contract or of reflection aiming at the assurance of common welfare" nor was it given with the nation but anteceded it. It was actually expressed in "self-help" and in "national justice".[8]

Intuitive Wisdom

Menger feared the danger of arbitrary reforms, based on the intentions of the common will of a nation or its rulers, which were not the result of an "organic process" and did not therefore reflect the intuitive wisdom of organically developed social institutions.[9] Such arbitrary legislative acts led to a belief in authority unsupported by convictions based on the insight of individuals as to their interests, from which it had originally developed. "All institutions which sanctify law, even the philosophical systems which 'objectify' it or describe it as something 'above human wisdom' always benefit power".[10] By "human wisdom" Menger meant the very opposite of Keynes's wisdom of the chosen few.[11] For him human wisdom resulted from the freely interacting activities of individuals operating within the limits of a body of rules, customs, conventions and laws incorporating the social wisdom of a long process of trial and error. What he feared was similar to what F. A. Hayek has defined as "constructive rationalism". This "intentionalist or pragmatic" account of history resulted from the propensity to ascribe the origin of all institutions of culture to invention or design. Morals, religion and law, language and writing, money and the market were thought of as having been deliberately constructed by somebody, or, at least, as owing whatever perfection they possessed to such design. But as he so rightly again emphasized: the basic assumption underlying this belief is factually false. Many of the institutions of society are in fact the result of customs, habits or practices which have not been developed with such purposes in view and of whose origins we are unaware. For

Man is as much a rule-following animal as a purpose-seeking one. And he is successful not because he knows why he ought to observe the rules which he does observe, or is even capable of stating all these rules in words, but because his thinking and acting are governed by rules which have by a process of selection been evolved in the society in which he lives, and which are thus the product of the experience of generations.[12]

Thus for Simmel and for Menger, as also for most liberal economists of the nineteenth century, the monetary order was not something to be left to the whim of the Government or the State. Indeed, Menger pointed out that Governments had so often and so greatly misused their power that it was forgotten that a coin is nothing but a piece of metal the fineness and full weight of which was guaranteed by the mint. The fact that Governments had treated money as if it were merely the product of the convenience of men, and particularly of their legislatures, simply multiplied errors about its nature.[13]

Social Commitment

If then money neither arises from the edicts of the State nor can be left to its whims, on what "something" does it depend? There can, in my opinion, be no doubt that what they both had in mind was a certain disposition, willingness and aptitude in society which could be counted upon to ensure, as a matter of justice, the maintenance of the monetary order (and in normal circumstances the value of money) through law or custom. For, as Menger emphasized, law not only arose from the mind of the people but depends on them for its realization. "It is affirmed in tradition and in the custom of even-handed dealing".[14] It is on this that the trust and confidence – which are the essence of money – rest. In other words, I would say that in the last resort the monetary order depends on the moral ideology of society.

I would emphasize at this point that, as Preston King has so well expressed it, "an ideology involves both some manner of deduction from an overriding principle and some sort of commitment to an exclusive goal. It may involve more of one than the other, but more of either one, rather than of any one in particular. It involves commitment as part of a political process.[15]

The same point was made by John Rawls: having a morality "is analogous to having made a firm commitment in advance; for one must acknowledge the principles of morality even when to one's disadvantage. A man whose moral judgements always coincided with his interests could be suspected of having no morality at all."[16]

The view that it is society's responsibility to maintain trust in the money of the realm is the backdrop of the professional debates among economists during most of the nineteenth century. The classical economists generally took this for granted as part of the reaction to the excesses of the French experiences. Memories of these for long continued to send shudders through the capitals of Europe.

A Credit Theory of Money

There were many others who stressed the importance of monetary order. Ond of these was the undeservedly neglected pioneer in the theory of banking and credit Henry Dunning Macleod,[17] who was more aware of the implications of the issues involved than most of his contemporaries.[18] He foresaw the continually growing significance which debts would assume in economically sophisticated communities. He realized that debt could, given the appropriate institutional background, be used *as if* it were money. This led him to make an attempt to "develop a credit theory of money as possibly preferable to a monetary theory of credit."[19] He preferred "the fundamental conception of money as being the *Representative of Debt* to that of its being the *Measure of Exchange*":[20] as money evolved the greater became the importance of the "fiduciary" or confidence factor. Although his language was sometimes confused this was what, I believe, he had in mind when he suggested that money is the highest and *most general* form of credit.[21]

Thus, long before Simmel or Carl Menger at the end of the century, he was concerned with the question: what brings about the general acceptability of money? "A right to demand something from an individual", he wrote, "has only particular value, and as the individual may not be able to render that something, its value is precarious, but as money is exchangeable among *all* persons at *all* times and in *all* places of the same country, its value is permanent and general." And why is this so? As the answer he quotes the following passage from Bastiat[22] concerning the "true function of money":

You have a crown piece. What does it mean in your hands? It is, as it were, the witness and the proof, that you have at some time done some work, which instead of profiting by, you have allowed society to enjoy, in the person of your client. This crown piece witnesses that you have rendered a service to society, and moreover it states the value of it. It witnesses besides, that you have not received back from society a *real* equivalent service, as was your right. To put it in your power to exercise this right when and how you please, society by the hands of your client, has given you an *Acknowledgement*, a *Title*, an *Order of the State*, a *Token*, a *Crown piece*, . . . and if you can read with the eye of the mind, the inscription it bears, you can distinctly see these words "*Pay to the bearer a service equivalent to that which he has rendered to society, value received and stated, proved, and measured by that which is on me."*[23]

This romantic eulogy may jar on modern ears. Yet it raises one of the neglected issues of our time: the nature and significance of trust in money. This I propose to consider next.

Trust and Character

What meaning can be ascribed to trust? What is its social significance? Trust and faith have been defined as assured reliance on some person or thing; as a confident dependence on the character, ability, strength or truth of someone or something.

Personal trust can be said to be based on the belief that the person will honour an obligation, and he will keep a promise, under all circumstances over which he has control. It is trust in this sense which is the binding cement of all contractual relationships. Whether unforeseen circumstances are likely to arise which could prevent the fulfilment of promises or obligations, through no fault of the parties concerned, is not a question of trust but of probability. That is the essential difference between a debt and an investment. The first involves a promise, the second only the expectation of a return.

When we trust a person, we are going beyond the mere assessment of probabilities. Indeed, trust or mistrust takes its place precisely because such an assessment cannot easily be made, or because it is too costly or time-consuming to attempt to do so. It enters where more exact knowledge is not available.

Trust rests on our idea of the character or nature of the person confronting us. For instance:

... We ascribe to people traits of character like honesty, punctuality, considerateness and meanness. Such terms do not, like ambition or hunger or sexual desire, indicate the sorts of goals that a man tends to pursue; rather they indicate the type of regulation that he imposes on his conduct whatever his goals may be. A man who is ruthless, selfish, punctual, considerate, persistent, and honest, does not have any particular goals; rather he pursues whatever goals he has in particular sorts of ways.[24]

Simmel had this in mind when he wrote[25] that to say one believes in someone, without adding thereto or even thinking what one really believes of him is a very fine and subtle turn of language. It is just the feeling that, from the very beginning, there exists between our idea of a being and this being itself a connection, a unity, a certain consistency of our picture of him – and the willingness to accept it – which, no doubt, rests on specific grounds but does not consist of them.

Trust is like love. To attempt to obtain it by bribery or purchase is to debase, indeed, to destroy it; an age-old truth – immortalized in *King Lear*.[26] When we trust a person, we assume that he will not voluntarily be false to that trust to serve his own interest. That assumption is based on our assessment of the kind of person he appears to be, or is supposed to be, or the customary role he is fulfilling. One might trust a man with one's wife but not with one's car. Even if the man possessed a certificate of competency as a motor-mechanic, other problems of trust would remain. Was he likely to use the car for his own pleasure without permission? To drive it recklessly, and the like?

Trust and Social Communication

Our information concerning persons or institutions is always relatively limited. Individuals and societies are dependent on countless symbols, myths, beliefs and institutions which function as indicators of trustworthiness or the opposite. That is why trust has been described as a means of reducing complexity and a form of social communication. Notwithstanding all attempts at organization, planning, and so forth, it is impossible to attempt to control all social action on the basis of expectations which can be calculated with certainty. There always remain uncertainties which must be absorbed by individuals or institutions whose role it is to do so. The right course of action cannot be known accurately enough in advance. It can only be known after and not before it is embarked upon. But decisions have to be made and actions undertaken before and not after the event. The complexity this involves is reduced through trust, which spans the problems of time and uncertainty.

One person trusts another to master an unforeseeable situation or one which he cannot understand or deal with. By doing so the complexity of the world of the future is reduced for him. Thus he who acts on trust has a better chance of success.[27]

Through trust one avoids having to take account of some possibilities. One neutralizes certain dangers which cannot be eliminated but which should not be permitted to disturb the taking of action or the embarking on an enterprise. However, the reduction of complexity, in this sense, is not deduction. Trust, as Simmel noted, is, in the final resort, unprovable. It is a mixture of knowledge and non-knowledge.[28]

Money, in terms of modern functional analysis, has come to be regarded – just as have power or truth – as a symbol of communication by means of which social complexity is reduced.[29] Thus Luhmann rightly stresses that the belief that the money-mechanism ensures decentralized freedom of individual decision-making rests on the postulate that money really does enjoy trust. Simmel saw this clearly. For him functional abstract money grows out of trust as social custom, remains embedded in it, and, one could say, is almost sanctified by it. Unless people had trust in one another, he wrote, society itself would fall apart. Few relationships are really based only on what the one knows about the other. Few relationships would last for even a short time if faith were not as strong as, and often stronger than, rational proofs or appearances. Without trust the monetary system would break down.

Personal and Generalized Trust

As Luhmann has expressed it in modern terms, the rational pursuit of advantage through round-about methods of production, postponement of consumption, saving etc. can only be motivated when the disturbing influences of the *incalculable* actions of others can be eliminated through trust. Luhmann is at one with Simmel in recognizing that such trust implies that he who believes in the stability of the value of money, and in the continuance of a multiplicity of uses for it, is basically assuming the existence of a functioning system. Such a system institutionalizes trust in money. It creates a kind of certainty and equivalence. In current economic terminology, "liquidity" comes to be regarded as a means of economizing on information.

However, it is well for us to remember Simmel's warning that, in the last resort, it is not the systems, but the individuals who operate them, that have to be trusted. It is not enough to point to the fact[30] that personal trust is converted, under the conditions of modern civilization, to generalized trust in the ability of systems to maintain circumstances and performance within certain limits: that trust depends on a reflex willingness to accept fictions because they function. As Berger and Luckmann have emphasized:[31]

Because they are historical products of human activity, all socially constructed universes change, and the change is brought about by the concrete actions of human beings. If one gets absorbed in the intricacies of the conceptual machineries by which any specific universe is maintained, one may forget this fundamental sociological fact. Reality is socially defined. But the definitions are always *embodied*, that is, concrete individuals and groups of individuals serve as definers of reality. To understand the state of the socially constructed universe at any given time, or its change over time, one must understand the social organization that permits the definers to do their defining. Put a little crudely, it is essential to keep pushing questions about the historically available conceptualizations of reality from the abstract "What?" to the sociologically concrete "Says who?"

Trust and the Monetary Economy

The trust in money – i.e. in who does the defining – therefore implies trust in the maintenance of the monetary order. This is not a question merely of how particular individual rights, debts, or obligations are dealt with. What is at issue here is a much more basic question: how can a trustworthy society, with stability of character be maintained and continue to be relied upon. In any individual case the law may not lead to a just decision but if laws generally are not justly applied then the system of law has broken down: law itself has been abrogated.

Similarly, a monetary economy implies the maintenance of a monetary order: one in which trade is conducted, in which debts and obligations are freely entered upon and discharged and services remunerated by money, the maintenance of the value of which is accepted by society, in its customs and laws, as its responsibility.

Whenever and wherever the use of money is restricted in relation to any existing or potential purpose, there is retrogression to a non-monetary economy in which political, authoritarian or barter transactions take the place of money. If money increasingly becomes an *instrument* of sectional political or economic action then it ceases to that extent to be inviolate in the sense of being guaranteed by society through its laws or customs. It is as if the

Supreme Court of the United States were to act as the mere instrument of the Executive through the person of the President. The constitution, and the system of laws and customs thereby established, which expresses the *character* of the American Society, would have been subverted.

In a free money economy individuals have to act on expectations as to how they will be permitted to consume or invest or hold money. However, such expectations are based on the twin assumptions that there will be a system of *money* contracts and a monetary system which bears an ordered relation to them. No individual has the right to expect that the laws governing property rights, or his rights as a consumer or producer, will always assume the same form. But the maintenance of a free monetary order implies that contracts freely made in money do, as such, carry society's guarantee that the measuring-rod of money in terms of which they are made will not be deliberately tampered with by anyone, *not even the Government itself*. As Keynes bluntly stated in one of his early books: "The individualistic capitalism of to-day, precisely because it entrusts saving to the individual investor and production to the individual employer, *presumes* a stable measuring-rod of value, and cannot be efficient – perhaps cannot survive – without one."

Significantly, in view of his later writings, he concluded in the next paragraph that "we must free ourselves from the deep distrust which exists against allowing the regulation of the standard of value to be the subject of *deliberate decision*". It is even more significant that he added "We can no longer afford to leave it in the category of which the distinguishing characteristics are possessed in different degrees by the weather, the birthrate, and the Constitution – matters which are settled by natural causes, or are the resultant of the separate action of many individuals acting independently, or require a revolution to change them."[32]

As I show in later chapters of this book, this conclusion is a *non sequitur*. The analogies used to support it are as unfortunate as they are revealing. The Constitution does not fall into the same category as the weather or as the resultant from the separate action of individuals. The Constitution incorporates a code of behaviour, of custom and of *principles*. It is not the result of a day-by-day, week-by-week or year-by-year series of deliberate *decisions* taken independently, but of decisions taken in terms of those principles and codes of behaviour and compatible with them.

In my opinion, therefore, when private individuals or institutions have, as now, to buy gold, commodities or foreign currency, to ensure greater security for themselves in the face of monetary and currency uncertainties, this is a sign of retrogression of and deterioration in the domestic monetary system. This may be due, first, to the deliberate rejection by the Government of any responsibility to maintain a free and secure monetary order. Second, it may result from the deliberate use of money "illusion" as an instrument of government policy. Third, it may result from weakness of the Government and its consequent inability to prevent special sections of the community from subverting monetary laws or customs for their own special purposes.

Whatever the particular circumstances or policies may be that undermine the trust in money, the consequence thereof is not in doubt: it is to undermine the continuance of the standard against which the free economic and social relations and aspirations of individuals are measured.

When Simmel referred, as I mentioned earlier, to money as the immovable mover what he had in mind was that money is the immovable standard which ensures free economic exchange and enterprise:[33] in the sense that trust facilitates known intercourse and faith moves mountains. In short, money is always in part an abstraction – one which portrays the character of society.

The Miser and the Spendthrift

It was in this abstract characteristic that Simmel saw the Achilles heel of any functionally advanced monetary system. A high degree of abstraction was very likely to engender profound misconceptions concerning the nature of money. It caused it to be regarded as possessing powers of its own, instead of merely reflecting or expressing *cost and value relationships*.

Simmel illustrates the most extreme misconceptions concerning the power of money by the respective attitudes of the miser and the spendthrift.[34] Both reject the valuation of the utility of money in terms of other things than itself. Both attempt to escape from the reality that money itself is nothing: that it has ultimately always to be translated into specific ends and into concrete objects or services. In his desire to escape from reality the miser regards the not spending of money as constituting its definite and satisfying value. He does not regard money as a means to anything else or to anything in particular. For the miser all goods lie on the periphery of existence. As, and when, money has to be translated into the enjoyment of concrete things its power and attraction are for him dissipated.

As opposed to the attitude of the miser that of the spendthrift exhibits a swing to the other extreme. His actions are not based on the power yielded by keeping money but on that of getting rid of it. His enjoyment consists in the act of spending as such: be it on anything whatsoever. What characterizes his actions is not that he irrationally disposes of his money as such but that he uses it for irrational purposes, i.e. in a manner that bears no relation to the circumstances in which he in reality finds himself. The desire of the moment blinds the spendthrift alike to the immediate value of money and to the real ends which it represents in relation to the future. His actions are as exaggerated and limitless as those of the miser. Whereas the miser projects the value of possessing money into infinity, the spendthrift does the opposite, by regarding the immediate here and now as the scene of apparently *limitless* experience, without thought for the morrow.

Obviously, these are illustrations of extreme psychological states and are treated by Simmel as such. We must pay heed to the context in which they occur. They are discussed in relation to the danger of any form of abstracting from reality and from the exigencies of life with its constant burdens and responsibilities of cost and choice in terms of the past and the future. We cannot seek in money the power either of the miser or the spendthrift to deliver what is beyond its province. For money has not the power to deliver anything – only society can do that.

Simmel was concerned about the danger – so difficult to avoid – of regarding the monetary order in purely abstract terms: specifically the danger that by doing so we would expect either too much or too little from it.

In the inflationary times of the present it is not, unfortunately, difficult to find examples of the influence and the danger of such abstractions be they in the form of excessive hoarding, owing to individual fears of continuing social instability, or in the form of irrational individual or social spending to grasp the joys of the fleeting moment.

CHAPTER IV

The Nominalist Dissent

... the Age of Chartalist or State Money was reached when the State claimed the right to declare what thing should answer as money to the current money-of-account – *when it claimed the right not only to enforce the dictionary but also to write the dictionary*. To-day all civilised money is, beyond the possibility of dispute, chartalist. J. M. Keynes.[1]

A Dictionary of Money

The above quotation from J. M. Keynes contains a Freudian slip which is as significant as the passage in which it occurs. It is not true that the State or any other authority can either enforce or write a dictionary, even if it wished to do so.

A dictionary is not created by an author like a novel or a scientific work. A dictionary is a collection of words which *society* has created in the past and is continuously creating and re-creating in the present and the future. Nobody has ever been able to force a single word on to society which the individuals composing it did not wish to use. A language "... is something that can only grow in and be *sustained* by a community".[2]

As a distinguished medical researcher has written:

We are born knowing how to use language. The capacity to recognize syntax, to organize and deploy words into intelligible sentences, is innate in the human mind. We are programmed to identify patterns and generate grammar. ... As chicks are endowed with an innate capacity to read information in the shapes of overhanging shadows, telling hawks from other birds, we can identify the meaning of grammar in a string of words, and we are born this way. ... We work at this all our lives, and collectively we give it life, but we do not exert the least control over language, not as individuals or committees or academies or governments.[3]

The passage from Keynes which I have quoted at the head of this chapter is preceded by the following:

The State, therefore, comes in first of all as the authority of law which enforces the payment of the thing which corresponds to the name or description in the contract. But it comes in doubly when, in addition, *it claims the right to determine, and declare what thing corresponds to the name, and to vary its declaration from time to time – when, that is to say, it claims the right to re-edit the dictionary. This right is claimed by all modern States and has been so claimed for some four thousand years at least. It is when this stage in the evolution of Money has been reached that Knapp's Chartalism – the doctrine that money is peculiarly a creation of the State – is fully realised.*[4]

The confusions in this passage demand examination. They are similar to those which A. I. Melden has suggested arise from attempts "to translate locutions about rights into locutions about what it is right to do, and the best that can be said for this way of speaking . . . is that it simply ignores those areas of moral discourse in which we speak of a right which one person has *as against another* and, correlatively, the obligation which the latter has *to* the former. For what it substitutes for this language of rights is the different albeit related discourse about what it is right to do. It is this confusion . . . that mars . . . much of the current talk about rights as claims".

But what does it mean to say that the State *"claims the right"* to declare what thing should answer as money? Claim from whom? Answerable to whom? Such questions involve the discussion of rights and obligations. The mere assertion that the state or community claims a right is not very helpful.

"A right, we are often told, is a claim," continues Melden.[5] This, he points out, presumably means that a person might have a right without registering a claim, but, he asks, "What on earth is a claim one does not make? Clearly it can only be a right, and of course the word 'claim' is often used in legal contexts as a synonym for 'right'; but in that case we have not advanced a single jot." Nor does it help to argue that one must "distinguish" claims that are justified, and which, as justified, are rights, from claims that stand in need of such justification and are not entitled, in consequence, to being designated as "rights".

I cannot here enter upon the details of his further analysis but must content myself with quoting his conclusion that "attempted 'reductions' of statements about rights into statements about right action do violence to the actual procedures of moral reflection. . . . Agents have rights. Rights compete for moral satisfaction. Moral wisdom consists not only in recognizing that a right may operate as a consideration that supports the claim that an action is right, but also in recognizing how to weigh such supporting considerations whenever they compete and how in such cases to arrive at a determination of what it is that one is morally required to do".

He finally concludes: "What, however, is meant by the 'rightness', the 'moral requiredness' of an action, and how does this feature connect with the manner in which an action serves this moral structure? Here I shall be very brief: It is self-evident – analytic – that it is right that one maintains the moral community of which one is a member. To be right is the very same thing as to be the kind of action that does serve, however that may be, the moral community. There is no further feature over and above this one that is the rightness and that needs to be connected with it."[6]

Double Talk about Debt

It is necessary, however, to pursue this matter a little further. It will be remembered that Keynes defined Money-Proper as that the delivery of which will discharge a contract or a debt and Bank-Money as simply an acknowledgement of a *private* debt used alternately with Money-Proper to settle a transaction. However, Bank-Money could also, he argued, represent ". . . a debt owing by the State; and *the State may then use its chartalist prerogative to declare that the debt itself is an acceptable discharge of a liability.*[7] . . . When, however, what was merely a debt has become Money-Proper, it has changed its character and should no longer be reckoned as a debt, since it is of the essence of a debt to be enforceable in terms of something other than itself. . . ." Keynes then suggested that: "At the cost of not conforming entirely with current usage, I propose to include as State-Money not only money which is itself compulsory legal tender but also money which the State or the Central Bank undertakes to accept in payments to itself or to exchange for compulsory legal-tender money".

The idea that a debtor, and particularly the State or Government finding itself in that position, could claim to *discharge a debt by merely declaring what should be regarded as discharging it* is surely very odd. A debt has not been discharged by a *declaration* that it has been paid – it can only be discharged by paying it. If the State or others have "discharged" it by a legal fiction it has not been paid – it has been abrogated. It is a peculiar use of language – a form of double-talk – to suggest that a promise can be kept by another promise to keep it at a later date in an infinite progress of promises: such promises have not been kept. Their fulfilment has only been postponed.

If a promise to repay a debt is postponed, the debt remains undischarged for the time being. It is true that a further debt may be voluntarily *accepted*, in lieu of the repayment of the original debt, but this is not the *fulfilment* of a contract but the making of a new one. If this is brought about by compulsion, we are back to the position that the debt has, in effect, not been honoured. I assert that the idea that the State can, as of right, abrogate debts in this way by *declaring* them to be "money" fails to take into account the moral context in terms of which, in a free society, they arise.

The Moral Situation

In my opinion, the fact that a debt represents a *promise* from the debtor to the creditor, or his successors in title, is crucial. A. I. Melden has used the example of the decision of umpires in the game of cricket to elucidate the moral issue involved. The umpires' decisions and the subsequent action of players have to be related to the way of thinking and acting that constitute the playing of the game. Only thus can we understand the motives provided by the decisions which the umpires make. However, he suggests "that there are considerable differences between umpires' decisions and promises. In the case of promises there are no formalized rules to the effect that when one says 'I promise . . .' the person to whom one addresses this utterance will be assured and will act accordingly. . . . Again, we are not engaged in the playing of a game when we promise – a game which we might choose as our fancy suits us, to play or not to play – we are engaged in a moral transaction, indifference to which is indifference to the requirements of moral integrity."

Nevertheless, Melden insists, there is an important analogy between promises and the playing of a game. "Just as we need to relate umpires' decisions and the subsequent actions of players to that relatively enduring way of thinking and acting that constitutes the playing of a game in order that we may understand the motives provided by umpires' decisions, so we need to relate promise utterances and the motivations these provide for those to whom they are addressed to the enduring moral context in which they are made. For not only do I signify my intention or resolution, my conviction that I can and shall perform the described action, I also *present* myself as a moral agent whose moral reputation and continuing moral relations with the person to whom I promise are at stake in the performance of the action. This I am able to do because I *connect* the performance of the action promised with my status as a morally responsible agent – to promise is to signify though not to assert, that one has tied his status as a moral agent to the performance of the action in question."[8]

Moreover, it is important to notice, as H. L. A. Hart[9] has shown, that the moral situation which arises from a promise does not justify the identification "of having a right" with benefiting by the performance of a "duty". "It is important for the whole logic of rights that, while the person who stands to benefit by the performance of a duty is discovered by considering what will happen if the duty is not performed, the person who has a right (to whom performance is *owed* or *due*) is discovered by examining the transaction or antecedent situation or relations of the parties out of which the "duty" arises. . . . Perhaps some clarity on this matter is to be gained by considering the force of the preposition "to" in the expression "having a duty to Y" or "being under an obligation to Y" (where "Y" is the name of a person); for it is significantly different from the meaning of "to" in "doing something to Y" or "doing harm to Y" where it indicates the person affected by some action. In the first pair of expressions, "to " obviously does not have this force, but indicates the person to whom the person morally bound is bound. This is an intelligible development of the figure of a bond (*vinculum juris: obligare*): the precise figure is not that of two persons bound by a chain, but of *one* person bound, the other end of the chain lying in the hands of another to use if he chooses."[10]

Notwithstanding Keynes's frequent appeals to morality, his claim that all "civilised money" is chartalist and is "a creation of the State" is in effect a claim to place discussion of the nature, meaning and significance of money outside moral discourse and beyond the moral structure of a free community. A possible reason for the claim is because Keynes fails to make an adequate distinction between the power of the State and the institutional evolution of society: between the role of Government and the role of custom. I am not deterred from this view by the fact that at times he appears to use the terms State and Community interchangeably. What is far more significant is that Keynes, in claiming *"beyond the possibility of dispute"* that to-day all *"civilised"* money is chartalist, quoted from, and referred with specific approval to, the highly legalistic views of Georg Friedrich Knapp.

Monetary Nominalism

Knapp's main contention was that money is essentially the creation of law and wholly a State affair. Money was to be regulated by the State entirely in its own interest. The value of money is secondary: what is important is its validity, by which he meant its power to discharge debt. In his opinion this power was given to money solely by the State.

The monetary unit is, according to Knapp,[11] purely "nominal". The franc, the dollar, and the florin do not connote a fixed weight of metal. They are abstract units.

Once a money has been established, it can only be changed by an admission of the nominal character of the monetary unit; *this character consists in the possibility of the State changing the means of payment, while the relative magnitude of different debts remains unchanged*.

Whatever else one may think of these definitions of money one thing is certain – they are not based on any particular moral conception. They are formal, juridical or, as Knapp says, "historical". Significantly, Keynes appealed to history in precisely the same manner in the quotation I have given on page 44 above. I believe that this conception of money is fallacious and that it has had and continues to have a very deleterious influence on monetary thought and policy.

I give below two examples of the subtle or unconscious way in which this nominalist conception of money, and the power of the State or monetary authorities in relation thereto, has penetrated current thought. The first is in an article by Gail Pearson[12] in which the statement is made: "Despite the historical connection to a medium of exchange, however, credit-creating systems may be devised without one. *All that is necessary* is community agreement to *establish* such a system – for example, the current international monetary arrangement involving Special Drawing Rights." The ultimate sophistication was described by Schumpeter as simply the "creation of new purchasing power out of nothing". (J. A. Schumpeter, *The Theory of Economic Development*, Oxford University Press, 1961, p. 73.)

Unfortunately in real life nothing can be created out of nothing. Credit is not something which can be created at will. It always rests finally on trust: on the *belief* that the borrower will produce or cause to be produced or come into possession of the wherewithal to keep his promise to re-pay what has been borrowed. Symptomatic of current views is Gail Pearson's belief that through the use of a medium of exchange "a source of purchasing power has been introduced that is independent of current and expected future resources" because "the monetary authorities can lend this purchasing power at will (or supply the reserves for intermediaries to do so)". She argues that the recipients of it can, by purchasing the excess output or by bidding up the prices of resources, generate forced saving. This she regards as "the credit creation function of money".[13] However, it is significant that she adds: "Thus the role of monetary policy in the framework of both Keynes and Schumpeter is to *anticipate* the needs to keep the economy at full employment and to be flexible enough to meet the credit needs for growth. If this is to be done without inflation, variations in aggregate saving through interest rate policies or through the budget have to be achieved."

But this is to admit that, far from a new source of purchasing power having been introduced which is "independent of current and expected future resources", monetary authorities are confronted with exactly the same circumstance on which all credit rests – trust and judgement. It is to admit that the claims which the monetary authorities establish by the promise to pay the creditor require the production by society of the means to honour them. These claims imply, as Gail Pearson admits, that their promises will not be regarded as merely nominal and will not be abrogated by "paying" them in depreciated currency. But this involves the successful use of the credit which appears to be created independently. Promises can create nothing except through the subsequent action of society. When the real social interrelations between individuals, which underlie these actions, are misjudged the promises cannot be kept. If, nevertheless, monetary authorities or Governments consciously try to create credit, knowing that their actions will lead to the debasement of the currency, they only succeed in fostering uncertainty and mistrust.

Gail Pearson, in keeping with many others, is, of course, quite right in stressing the beneficial effects of highly sophisticated monetary systems which permit the development and refinement of debt and credit relationships. But, as I show later, a system of institutions which permits personal trust to operate cannot replace it. Trust is not a mechanical artifact.

This consideration brings me to my second example which I quote from Lachmann,[14] who wrote:

Modern money consists of claims against banks, central banks, or governments. It is of the essence of such a system that the total number of such claims that might be created is in principle unlimited, though control by a public authority may limit it at any particular point of time. While in the world of 1920 it was possible to hold that the limited quantity of metallic money kept the price system within bounds and thus also set limits to the maximum wage-rates attainable by bargaining, no such "ultimate determinant" exists at the present time. Today it would be almost more correct to say that the total quantity of money-claims is influenced by nothing so much as by the total amount of wage-claims that have been granted. This is what Sir John Hicks meant by the "labour standard" which has replaced the old gold standard. In other words, the transition from a metallic to a credit standard, the adoption of a monetary system in which money can be created virtually at will, has removed an important external restraint on the wage-setting power of the industrial bargainers.

Unfortunately money does not consist of claims but is the means of settling them by what it will purchase, and that cannot be "created" by monetary institutions or by the State "at will" but only – to repeat – by society's successful production of the things which money can buy. The granting of wage-claims, for example, is one thing, what wages will purchase is quite another. To speak of a "labour-standard" of value is indeed a striking way of drawing attention to its deficiencies. So too one could speak of making a standard out of elastic – but nobody would think of relying on it.

Knapp's definition of money as purely chartalist, i.e. as being only the creation and creature of the State, rests on a category mistake similar to that to which I have already referred.[15] For Simmel, the State is but one part of society and society is a process, not a thing. The State cannot determine the monetary process, no more than it can determine the activities of the whole society through it. Money, therefore, should not be regarded as some extra member additional to society, any more than any economic activity should be so regarded.

Unfortunately, we easily and frequently fall into that very error: regarding money as if it were a power or force in its own right by means of which we can do anything and everything. We make the same mistake when we think that money and capital can do anything. We forget that behind those abstract terms lies an ever-changing world of inescapable institutional arrangements. They are part of that reality which constantly breaks in upon our abstract calculations, as it disrupts our day-dreams, hopes and prognostications. As I have written elsewhere,[16] capital like technology is:

apart from the symbolism of accounting, always "concrete" in the sense that it is embedded in, and attuned to, the particular purposes and state of knowledge which led to its "creation". It is but temporarily incorporated in ever changing forms and patterns suited to the evanescent ends for which it is designed. It is a social heritage dependent upon the institutions and habit-patterns of thought and action of individuals in society.

This is the basic reason why capital cannot be "stored-up" for long. It cannot be transferred from one situation to another without the individuals who will re-adapt and re-fashion it for use in a new pattern of activity. For no two situations, no two regions, no two societies, no two problems of choice, in time or place, are alike. In this sense capital is like technical "know-how", which also does not exist in the abstract ready to be applied to any new situation. To transfer "know-how" is not to apply something which is known. It is to apply new ways of thinking to find out what is not known: as when research is undertaken to develop new crops; discover the nature of soils; prospect for minerals; adapt old aptitudes to new skills; and perfect machines for new tasks. It is because existing forms in which knowledge, i.e. capital, is incorporated are no longer suitable that the old has constantly to be fashioned anew in attempts to meet the future. Capital is, as has been repeatedly said, a means of saving time but it is only possible to save time if one can discover the purpose to which one will devote it.

Knapp himself seemed to be aware of this reality when he pointed out that national currencies can lose value because of their inability to prove "fungible" beyond national frontiers – i.e. in common parlance – when they are no longer accepted. This of course can happen against the "will" of the State, even within its own boundaries, when the "creation" of money ceases to be related to the realities of its social and economic circumstances. At a time of world inflation it is hardly necessary to describe such circumstances in detail here.

What, I suggest, Knapp's and all similar chartalist or nominalist theories of money have in common is that they are finally self-defeating. For if we grant the basic assumption on which they all rest: that the State is all-powerful in monetary affairs, that it can and should *decree* what money is and is to be, how it shall be used and who may and who may not use it, then we have in fact assumed away a free monetary order.

The abolition of a free monetary order has, of course, been advocated by opponents of a free society for a very long time. It has been achieved to all intents and purposes in most communist countries. But the legalistic Knapp was not thinking of a communist society at all. When it came to the crunch he was quite agonisingly aware of the practical limitations of his "State Theory of Money". He had to admit that the need and essential object of the principal monetary systems was to establish a fixed rate of exchange with the chief commercial countries; and in particular with England – the largest buyer and seller of goods. Thus he wrote: "Nothing is further from our wishes than to seem to recommend paper money pure and simple . . . it is well for any State to wish to keep to specie money and to have the power to do so. And I know of no reason why, under normal circumstances, we should depart from the gold standard."

"To have the power to do so" – there's the rub. How does the State get the power – not to mention here the inconvenient little other matter, namely, the knowledge to do so – without destroying freedom of exchange in a free monetary order? As Rist pointed out: "Knapp looks at the question from the standpoint of power: what he does not explain is why so many states want to be bound to the English standard, is it not precisely because of its stability and continuity, arising less from the power of England than from a certain conception of money.''[17]

He rightly drew attention to the fact that basically it was not the political or strategic power of Britain that ensured the stability of her money but the power of her social institutions which, in monetary affairs, ensured that Government should be subject to them and to the rule of law in order that the stability and continuity of the monetary standard in terms of gold should be maintained.

It was a conception, as we have seen, that rested on certain customs of integrity: a sense of probity, adherence to a strict code of behaviour in monetary affairs and the belief that honesty or faith secures order in the industrial world.[18] Such a view is contrary to the very idea that the value of money is due to its being accepted by the State in payment of debts at values to be decided and varied at its will.[19]

Already Carl Menger had exposed the inadequacy of juridical views on money which were sometimes espoused by economists, who attempted to include in the concept of money the coercive powers of the State. He drily remarked that ''forced currency'' mostly has the purpose of compelling people to use it against their will. It was, he suggested, an even greater error to assert that the fiat of the State should be regarded as an indispensable characteristic of money. The contrary was the truth. Experience had shown that the money of the country would prove the more acceptable the less it required force for its acceptance. For, in so far as it was not merely regarded in formal juridical terms, a forced currency always implied legal compulsion on the creditor to accept in payment of his monetary claims (and sometimes of other claims also) kinds of money which deliberately, or implicitly, did not correspond to the agreed contents of his claims or did not correspond to their value in the free market. He illustrated the absurdity of the idea that money could really depend on force – an idea which to him seemed almost incredible – from the debate at that time as to whether a bank-note was really money at all. Menger pointed out that those who would deny that the notes of a *solvent* bank are money would – as *true believers in the virtues and indispensability of legal force in currency matters* – assert that if the bank were to go bankrupt the very same notes would become real money if they were then merely declared to be legal tender by the State![20] This example, adequately up-

dated, is not, I suggest, without significance in relation to current
international monetary debates.

As Robert Giffen wrote:

No change in a monetary standard, if it is a tolerably good one, ought to be
proposed or considered unless upon grounds of overwhelming necessity.
For a good money is so very difficult a thing to get, and Governments, when
they meddle with money, are so apt to make blunders (and have, in fact,
made such blunders without end in the past, . . .) that a nation which has a
good money should beware of its being tampered with, and especially
should beware of any change in the foundation – the standard for money.
Locke, and other older economists, went further, and maintained that a
change of standard should *never* be made, because every change involves
injustice. But without going so far as this, we may recognise that there are
various practical reasons for not changing lightly or readily – that is, for not
changing for any other reasons than those of overwhelming necessity.
These considerations apply especially to the standard for money in a
country like England, where the standard is the foundation of a fabric of
credit, whose extension and delicacy make the slightest jar apt to produce
the most formidable effects.[21]

It is worth adding that Giffen was quite clear as to what he meant
by a monetary standard. There was to be no monkeying around with
it or mincing of words about it. He made it clear in his objection to
the tabular standard. He wrote: "It is necessary to a good monetary
standard that the thing which is the standard should itself be the
medium in which payments are made, or that the medium should
consist of currency readily convertible into the thing which is standard, whereas the proposed standard, consisting really of quantities
of a great many articles, could never be seen or handled."

Giffen was writing at the time of the controversies about
bimetallism. It is interesting to note the main reason for the stand he
took on that issue. "In their recent arguments against bimetalists
some of my friends", he pointed out,

have dwelt very strongly on the importance to us of maintaining our gold
standard, because the standard has appreciated when measured by commodities, and there is a great deal due to us as a community in gold. But I
should not put the argument that way. What impresses me is that, with our
enormous liabilities and credits, with transactions of all kinds, the ramifica-
tions of which no man can follow out, all based on a gold standard, we can
never tell, when we touch that standard, what confusion and mischief we
may be introducing.

What he had in mind by "confusion and mischief" is shown by his attitude to paper money. He could not understand how the *"automatic regulation"* of it by "an issuing institution" is possible. Sometimes he thought much "paper" will be wanted . . . at other times less . . . no issuing body can force it, though the attempt at forcing may produce disastrous results.

Of particular relevance today is his conclusion that:

It would facilitate further study of the subject, if, in the case of so novel a proposal, those who make it, instead of writing of "paper" *in the abstract, would give a specimen of one of their notes, so that one may see what is promised, who makes the promise and so on.* I cannot help thinking that the writing of a specimen note in this case would have brought out some of the difficulties of the undertaking.[22]

It is surely ironic that, after a hundred years, no less a monetary authority than Milton Friedman should, almost in despair, recommend the tabular standard for a very different reason in the form of escalator clauses based on indexation of contracts, debts, wages etc. It will be brought about by legislation for Government, leaving it voluntary for the rest of the economy.[23] His proposal is based on the dangers of a runaway inflation or an authoritarian society, if present attitudes to money persist. He frankly states that the arrangements he proposes "involve *deliberately eschewing some of the advantages of the use of money*, and hence are not good in and of themselves. They are simply a lesser evil than a badly-managed money. The widespread use of escalator clauses would not by itself either increase or decrease the rate of inflation. But it would reduce the revenue that Government acquires from inflation – which also means that Government would have less incentive to inflate."

Thus his proposal is not made, as then, to improve a relatively dependable set of monetary institutions: a system based on trust, and one which had already curbed the power of Government, but in the hope that modern Governments, which are no longer subject to such restraints, will – as burglars might – be less inclined to rob us if their activities could somehow be made less profitable. Whether Milton Friedman's proposal will be generally adopted or, if it is, will be successful does not concern us here. What is significant is that he too thinks of the Government or the State as something additional, apart from or outside society whose attitude has to be tamed or counteracted. As, however, I have tried to show, it is in the change which has taken place in society as a whole – in its beliefs, goals and institutions – that we must seek for the causes and remedies for the monetary ills which beset us.

The ideology of trust, which I have examined in this and the previous chapter, was not based on the desire to further the special interests of particular individuals or economic groups, as Keynes suggested. On the contrary, it was concerned with money as a mark of the character of society: the degree of its certainty, dependability and credibility. Money was not considered to be a tool with which to make men behave justly, courageously or wisely, or indeed to behave in any particular manner at all. Rather that ideology rested on the belief that money could do none of these things.

What it was concerned with was that men should regard money as above suspicion because they realized that it could, finally, only reflect what society was. An old African proverb describes the point at issue precisely: "I cannot hear what you are saying because I see what you are." The ideology we have been examining was concerned that there should be as little difference as possible between what men said or promised about money and what it was seen to be by all who had to make use of it to express their rights, promises and obligations. In the next chapter we will encounter a very different philosophy.

CHAPTER V
The Keynesian Morality of Money

Rulers who design to purchase the assent of their subjects to the authority of *respublica* by the argumentative recommendation of the desirability
of its prescriptions, by instigations to subscribe, by negotiation with those of
their subjects who are disposed to disapprove (and there will always be
such), by bribes or benefactions, by cajolery, by indistinct promises of
better things to come, by reproach, encouragement, dissimulation, or
foreboding, in short, by the exercise of the art of persuasive leadership,
have ceased to be rulers and have become managers and there is no place
for them in civil association. Michael Oakeshott.[1]

Monetary Theology and Gold

J. M. Keynes reflected both consciously and unconsciously an
ambivalent attitude to money which has been deeply embedded in
European thought since the Middle Ages. This chapter examines
the nature of this dichotomy in Keynes's writings and those of many
of his successors. Its significance has been almost totally overlooked.

A Finance Minister of West Germany,[2] some years ago, expressed
the opinion that "the age of religious wars over monetary theology
appears to be ended". I fear that the Minister was somewhat over-
optimistic. The wars about monetary theology are not by any means
ended. They still affect what is, or should be, regarded as the very
purpose or function of money. The Finance Minister gave the
diminishing role of gold as an example of the ending of theological
monetary conflicts. But it is very doubtful whether the last chapter
in the monetary history of gold has been written. Certain aspects of
it also serve to illustrate the conflict in Keynes's thinking. I refer to
the controversy about "gold-hoarding" in India during which

Keynes for the first time had to deal with the conflict between the State and society: between abstract thought and social custom.

In his contribution to the "Conclusions" of the report of the Royal Commission on Indian Finance and Currency,[3] Keynes wrote: "If we take a larger view and look to the more remote future we are in sympathy with the school of thought which regards gold in circulation as essentially wasteful, and which holds that India should be encouraged in all reasonable ways to develop economical habits in matters of currency. In the long run the encouragement of the inclination to handle metallic coin must result in the locking up of much wealth in a barren form." Then came the dilemma: "But while educating the people in the use of more economical forms of currency, the Government should continue to act on the principle of *giving them the form of currency for which they ask*. . . . It is likely, moreover, that a long period will elapse before the growth of habits of banking can put an end to the existing demand for gold coins in hoards by taking their place as a means to make savings secure."[4] But, unfortunately for this view, he had to recognize that: "The line between gold in hoards and in circulation is an indefinable one, and the hoarding habit is sanctioned in India by the experience of centuries and by religious and racial laws and customs, with which the Government of India have neither the inclination nor the power to interfere."[5] He admitted that "The people of India have as much right to expend their resources without hindrance on the absorption of gold for such a purpose, as on any other object of luxury or distinction. Any attempt, therefore, to refuse gold would be likely to cause alarm and inconvenience, and unlikely to achieve its object." He continued (Par. 76): "There is, however, a clear line between meeting a definite demand for gold coins, which it would be unfair and impolitic to refuse, and encouraging a further demand for gold beyond what would exist otherwise."

What received no mention was the simple fact that gold-hoarding represented, as it to this day represents, a bulwark against the encroachment by Governments or rulers on individual freedom. From the point of view of millions of the people of India the precious metals were the only real money they could trust – as they had, and rightly, trusted it for millennia before in the face of succeeding conquerors and changing political circumstances. It was, in any case, their only means of personal insurance against uncertainty. It is likely that in India a reduction of hoarding would only have come from an increased sense of social and economic *security* rather than from deliberate attempts to restrict the use of gold.[6] Keynes's view concerning the barrenness of gold hoarding was misplaced. The fact that gold was hoarded in India simply showed that it was regarded by the people as the best form of *money* to protect their meagre savings.

Why did Keynes regard the hoarding of the precious metals as barren?

From Barrenness of Gold to Barrenness of Money

The answer to this question, I think, lies buried in the origins of European thought. From Plato and Aristotle onwards, and throughout the Middle Ages, there was little appreciation of the fact that trade is not the exchange of goods and services with *equivalent* values but that every exchange transaction creates *new* and additional gains over and above the values which existed before. Similarly it was not realized that through the holding of money balances, and thus facilitating the completion of exchange at a subsequent date, the precious metals increased the production of income beyond what was possible through direct barter. The precious metals were thus, when used as money, by no means barren.

Keynes came to extend the idea of the barrenness of gold to that of the barrenness of money. Paul Davidson drew attention to the fact that "Keynes was the first important economist to accuse bluntly the neo-classical view of the nature of money as foolish."[7] He was referring to the passage in the *Quarterly Journal of Economics* for February 1937[8] in which Keynes had written:

Money, it is well known, serves two principal purposes. By acting as a money of account it facilitates exchanges without its being necessary that it should ever itself come into the picture as a substantive object. *In this respect it is a convenience which is devoid of significance or real influence*. In the second place, it is a store of wealth. So we are told, without a smile on the face. But in the world of the classical economy, *what an insane use* to which to put it! *For it is a recognized characteristic of money as a store of wealth that it is barren*; whereas practically every other form of storing wealth yields some interest or profit. Why should anyone outside a lunatic asylum wish to use money as a store of wealth?[9]

Keynes answered his own question by stating that it was because, partly reasonably and partly instinctively, our desire to hold money is a barometer of the degree of our distrust of our calculations and conventions concerning the future. This feeling about money he regarded as instinctive, operating at a deeper level of our motivation when higher and more precarious conventions have weakened. "The possession of actual money lulls our disquietude; and the premium which we require to make us part with money is the measure of the degree of our disquietude."

On this Davidson correctly commented (in the article to which I refer above) "Distrust? Disquietude? These are states of mind impossible in a world of certainty (that is, in a world where the sum of the probabilities equals unity)."[10]

Keynes's Enigma

Uncertainty, however, is unfortunately not merely a state of mind. It is the human condition. He who would attempt to obviate uncertainty challenges not only fate but individual freedom also. That is the essence of the "quality of imperishable relevance to the essential, insoluble problems of time-bound humanity" which G. L. S. Shackle[11] finds in *The General Theory of Employment, Interest and Money*. He saw in it "the image of the vaster enigma of conduct, *decision* and history itself". He thought that Keynes's book achieves its triumph by pointing out that the problems it is concerned with "are essentially beyond solution" (p. 516).

Shackle is here criticizing also those who, in his opinion, wrongly regard Keynes's book as a "total" system – one which either *includes* any given element or else *assumes* its non-existence: in particular those[12] who remain within the professionally approved ground, "*the ground enclosed by the assumption that economic affairs are rational*". Keynes did not.

Earlier, Shackle had asked: "Why did Keynes try to answer the array of peculiar questions, *the questions about a system whose meaning and existence he was denying*? Can one doubt that he did so because he was asking these questions himself?" (p. 518).

And, in reply, Shackle quotes the last paragraph of the Preface to the General Theory in which Keynes had written, "The composition of this book has been for the author a long struggle of escape." Shackle adds, "He did escape; his critics did not."

But two questions remain: What exactly *did* Keynes try to escape from and if *he* escaped can *we* do likewise? It is the purpose of this chapter to deal with some of the issues these questions raise. It is significant that Shackle, in order to find some answers to what puzzled him, turned once again to Keynes's article in the *Quarterly Journal of Economics*, from which I have quoted. He describes it "as the canon which few economists seem able to endure the sight of". And why is this? It is because "it declares unequivocally that *expectations* do not rest on anything solid, determinable, demonstrable. 'We simply do not know' " (p. 516). Shackle concluded that the Keynesians were concerned with a model of economic society, an economic world, where knowledge of circumstance is *sufficient* – a model which Keynes repudiated, as an invented world, as totally alien to our real predicament. "We are not omniscient, assured masters of known circumstance via reason, but the prisoners of time" (p. 519). And why? Because, answers Shackle in defence of Keynes:

No one can make plans guaranteed to be realised and successful, who cannot consult Fate itself concerning its intended mockery of human ambitions. Futures markets? They can reconcile, just conceivably, our *present* ideas, based on our *present* knowledge. What of tomorrow's new knowledge, destroying the old or rendering it obsolete, what of tomorrow's choices and decisions, tomorrow's discoveries, tomorrow's inventions, work of imagination, tomorrow's output from the Cosmic Computer which may, after all, not be a computer but an ERNIE?[13]

The Replacement of Individual Choice

But it is worth pointing out that already in the early twenties Keynes was concerned with the possibility of bringing about another and very different world of thought and action. In this the allegedly puny fears and uncertainties of *free individuals* would no longer matter: they would be replaced by other decision-making processes and different decision makers.

In "The End of Laissez-faire"[14] Keynes is quite explicit about his general attitude to the freedom of the individual in economic affairs. He criticized doctrinaire State Socialism, not because it sought to engage men's altruistic impulses in the service of society or because it departed from *laissez-faire*, but because it was based on a misunderstanding of nineteenth-century State Socialism, which also sprang from Bentham and was really in some respects a more muddled version of just the same philosophy: "*Both equally laid all their stress on freedom*, the one negatively to avoid limitations on existing freedom, the other positively to destroy natural or acquired monopolies. They are different reactions to the same intellectual atmosphere"[15] (p. 291). The cure, he argued (p. 291), *lay outside the operations of individuals to whose interest it might even be "to aggravate the disease"*.

What is this disease? It is clear what Keynes had in mind. It was freedom of individual choice in the face of uncertainty. Indeed, he believed that the cure for these things was in part "to be sought in the deliberate control of the currency and of credit by a central institution, and partly in the collection and dissemination on a great scale of data relating to the business situation, including the full publicity, by law if necessary, of all business facts which it is useful to know. These measures would involve society in exercising *directive intelligence* through some appropriate organ of action over many of the *inner intricacies* of private business, . . ."[16] This passage throws light not only on Keynes's attitude towards uncertainty but on his despair concerning what he regarded as "the lack of knowledge and its total dominance of human affairs".[17] It illustrates, I believe, Keynes's approach to the problem, with which I deal below, of rationality in economic and business affairs. In that approach he falls into the type of error which Sir Karl Popper has called: "the bucket theory of science" (or "the bucket theory of mind") the persuasive doctrine that, before we can know or say anything about the world. we must first have had perceptions – sense experiences. "Our mind . . . resembles a container – a kind of bucket – in which perceptions and knowledge accumulate."[18]

As against this view, he contends that in science it is *observation* rather than perception which is decisive; but observation is an active process – one which is planned and prepared. We do not "have" an observation. We "make" an observation; it is always preceded by a particular interest – a question or a problem: by something theoretical.

What I wish to stress is that also in the world of practical economic affairs every new decision involving new enterprise rests on a similar need to ask a question, to observe afresh, to solve a problem, to experiment in regard to the as yet unformulated needs of consumers and the best methods for producers to meet them. Neither in the realm of science nor in the ordinary business of life does relevant knowledge lie ready to hand.

Another example of "directive intelligence" Keynes found in Savings and Investment. This he thought required some co-ordinated act of intelligent judgement as to the scale on which the community as a whole should save, which of these savings should go abroad in the form of foreign investments, and whether the market distributes savings along the rationally most productive channels. He did not specify who would make this intelligent judgement or how. As Keynes's biographer, Sir Roy Harrod, wrote so disarm-ingly, "he believed in the supreme value of *intellectual leadership, in the wisdom of the chosen few*".[19] As Keynes himself once said: "Words ought to be a little wild – for they are the assault of thoughts upon the *unthinking*." However he added: "*When the seats of power and authority have been attained, there should be no more poetic licence*."[20]

These attitudes, which Keynes retained to the end of his life, are not accidental. Indeed, they reflect an uneasiness similar to that which pervades Simmel's work on the inherent conflicts within the monetary economy. In Keynes, however, the unease results from quite different reasoning and rests on a different analysis. Moreover, the political commentator and innovator bursts through the bounds of philosophy to the formulation of social and economic policies, with startling and conflicting effects on his attitudes to the significance and consequence of the Monetary Economy it-self.

In order to understand the full import of these attitudes it is essential to look again at his classic book *The Economic Consequ-ences of the Peace*[21] which – like *The General Theory* – so well reflects not only his but our own perplexities.

Vision and Technique

It was Schumpeter who first drew attention to its significance to the whole of Keynes's subsequent work and thought, when he wrote:

In those pages of the Economic Consequences of the Peace we find nothing of the theoretical apparatus of the "General Theory". But we find the whole of the vision of things social and economic of which that apparatus is the technical complement. The General Theory is the final result of a long struggle to make that vision of our age analytically operative.[22]

In one sense, the book is a fiery tract of a young man attacking alleged wrongs about which he felt deeply; in another, it reflects the despair not of youth but of old age.

Haunting pessimism already marks the first paragraph of the introductory chapter:

The power to become habituated to his surroundings is a marked characteristic of mankind. Very few of us realise with conviction the intensely unusual, complicated, unreliable, temporary nature of the economic organisation by which Western Europe has lived for the last half century. We assume some of the most peculiar and temporary of our late advantages as natural, permanent, and to be depended on, and we lay our plans accordingly. On *this sandy and false foundation* we scheme for social improvement and dress our political platforms, pursue our animosities and particular ambitions, and feel ourselves with enough margin in hand to foster, not assuage, civil conflict in the European family.[23]

Symbolism and the Institutional Order

What "sandy and false foundation" was Keynes referring to in this revealing utterance – so at variance with the mood of trust and confidence of Bagehot and his contemporaries. After all, the maintenance of a symbolic universe is one of the essential pillars of the social construction of reality which is always in some sense "unusual, complicated, unreliable, and temporary". What society did Keynes have in mind which would not portray these features? What new recipe to ensure integrity and permanence in social relations? To quote again from Berger and Luckman (pp. 115–16):

Symbolic universes operate to legitimate individual biography and the institutional order. The operation is essentially the same in both cases. It is nomic, or ordering, in character. . . . Experiences belonging to different spheres of reality are integrated by incorporation in the same, overarching universe of meaning. . . . The provinces of meaning that would otherwise remain unintelligible enclaves within the reality of everyday life are thus ordered in terms of a hierarchy of realities, ipso facto becoming intelligible and less terrifying. This integration of the realities of marginal situations within the paramount reality of everyday life is of great importance, because these situations constitute the most acute threat to taken-for-granted, routinized existence in society. If one conceives of the latter as the "daylight side" of human life, then the marginal situations constitute a "night side" that keeps lurking ominously on the periphery of everyday consciousness. Just because the "night side" has its own reality, often enough of a sinister kind, it is a constant threat to the taken-for-granted matter-of-fact, "sane" reality of life in society. The thought keeps suggesting itself (the "insane" thought *par excellence*) that, perhaps, the bright reality of everyday life is but an illusion, to be swallowed up at any moment by the howling nightmares of the other, the night-side reality. Such thoughts of madness and terror are contained by ordering all conceivable realities within the same symbolic universe that encompasses the reality of everyday life – to wit, ordering them in such a way that the latter reality retains its paramount, definitive (if one wishes, its "most real") quality.

As Lachmann has pointed out, it is the function of social institutions to act as signposts; but the more often they are changed the less reliable they become as a means of orientation. Moreover there can be no permanence in a set of norms unless they are coherent.[24]

Consumed by terror of the night-side of Europe's culture, Keynes appears to have discounted completely the possible future effectiveness of the very factors which had made Europe the cultural and financial power-house of the world. This Europe he now described in words not of hope but of despair; suitable only as its epitaph. Yet he was fully aware of Europe's achievements, and the foundation on which they and, indeed, those of the United States of America still rested.

The Age of Faith

Nevertheless he wrote – in words that will always bear repetition:

What an extra-ordinary episode in the economic progress of man that age was which came to an end in August 1914: The greater part of the population, it is true, worked hard and lived at a low standard of comfort, yet were, to all appearances, reasonably contented with this lot. But escape was possible, for any man of capacity or character at all exceeding the average, into the middle and upper classes, for whom life offered, at a low cost and with the least trouble, conveniences, comforts, and amenities beyond the compass of the richest and most powerful monarchs of other ages. The inhabitant of London could . . . couple the security of his fortunes with *the good faith* of the townspeople of any substantial municipality in any continent . . . could secure . . . cheap and comfortable means of transit to any country or climate

without passport or other formality . . . and could then proceed abroad . . .
bearing *coined* wealth upon his person . . . But most important of all, he
regarded this state of affairs as normal, certain, and permanent, except in
the direction of further improvement, and any deviation from it as aberrant,
scandalous, and avoidable. The projects and politics of militarism and
imperialism, of racial and cultural rivalries, of monopolies, restrictions, and
exclusion, which were to play the serpent to this paradise, were little more
than the amusements of his daily newspaper, and appeared to exercise
almost no influence at all on the ordinary course of social and economic life,
the internationalisation of which was nearly complete in practice.[25]

The organization by which the peoples of Europe lived in that
happy age, when the Malthusian devil was chained up and out of
sight, and when currencies were maintained on a stable basis in
relation to gold and to one another, filled Keynes with admiration.[26]

The Capitalist Bluff

The serpent in this Garden of Eden which apparently accounted for
Keynes's pessimism was nothing other than the capitalist system
itself. Only a few pages later in the book is a section entitled "The
Psychology of Society"[27] in which fact gives way to fancy. The
remarkable system described in the passage quoted above, we are
told,

depended for its growth on a *double bluff or deception*. On the one hand the
labouring classes accepted from ignorance or powerlessness, *or were compelled, persuaded, or cajoled by custom, convention, authority, and the
well-established order of society* into accepting, a situation in which they
could call their own very little of the cake that they and nature and the
capitalists were co-operating to produce. And on the other hand the
capitalist classes were allowed to call the best part of the cake theirs and
were theoretically free to consume it, on the tacit underlying condition that
they consumed very little of it in practice.

There grew round the non-consumption of the cake, Keynes
alleged, all the instincts of puritanism and so the cake increased;
"*but to what end was not clearly contemplated*".[28] Individuals, he
argued, would be exhorted not so much to abstain as to defer and to
cultivate the pleasures of security and anticipation: the virtue of the
cake was that it was never to be consumed.

This picture of "a bourgoisie that kept on baking cakes in order not to eat them"[29] is misleading. It arises, of course, from Keynes's basic dissent from the "abstraction of a neutral money economy"[30] of the classical economists. In his own theories of unemployment, changes in the level of output are alleged to be due to the unwillingness of investors to invest in the circumstances assumed in his monetary theory of the effect of changes in the rate of interest. But theories of industrial fluctuation should not be permitted to obscure the fact that the processes of production of capital and consumption goods are basically interdependent and complementary. The idea that they are separate rests on a didactic abstraction from reality. The national cake was baked as one cake. Even though it might fluctuate in size or in the proportion of its ingredients of capital and consumption goods, the latter could not have been made available without the former, and vice versa.

There never was "a tacit underlying condition" that the capitalist consumed very little of the cake in practice. It was a figment of the imagination, like Jean Jacques Rousseau's "Social Contract". The capitalist system depended for its functioning not primarily on *inequality* of consumption but on those free, individual, contractual and credit relations in a *monetary* economy which made efficient saving, investment and consumption decisions possible. They did not result from decisions by Governments as to what level of saving would be "equitable" to *force* upon the people, as is the practice in authoritarian and communist countries.

It was precisely because the Victorian era believed that the devil of monetary deceit by Government had finally been chained up in civilized countries, that individuals ventured to inaugurate new combinations of the factors of production from which additional wealth flowed across the frontiers of the world.

The immense accumulations of fixed capital which were built up during the half-century before the First World War, Keynes alleged, could never have come about in a society where wealth was divided equitably. The railways of the world, which that age built as a monument to posterity, were, he thought, "not less than the Pyramids of Egypt, the work of labour which was not free to consume in immediate enjoyment the full equivalent of its efforts."[31] This analogy with the pyramids of Egypt is one which occurs frequently in Keynes's writings. It is false. The railways were not monuments to posterity but the arteries of the developing world of trans-continental effort which made that Europe possible which

Keynes had eulogized. They were not a symbol of dead accumulation but the carriers of the wherewithal which raised the current consumption of the men and women of Europe far above what it had been previously.

The analogy of the cake was unfortunate for another reason. "If only the cake were not cut," wrote Keynes, "but was allowed to grow . . . perhaps the day might come when there would at last be enough to go round, and when posterity could enter into the enjoyment of *our* labours. On that day overwork, overcrowding and underfeeding would come to an end, and men secure of the comforts and necessities of the body could proceed to the nobler exercises of their faculties."[32]

This overlooked that there was no way in which the cake could have been cut now and kept for the future by those who did not consume their portion. The portion which the savers *hoped* to be able to enjoy in the future could only be produced in the future and *then* shared out, in accordance with *contractual* arrangements with others, who would enable them, or their heirs, to obtain a piece of the future cake *then* being baked. The act of saving was thus an act of *trust* by the saver. He could relinquish to others the right to consume goods and services now, in exchange – not for *accumulated* goods and services – but for accumulated *obligations* by others to him which rested on *trust* in the debtor.

Psychological Motivations

Keynes's assessment of general psychological motivations in a money economy was even more erroneous. "I seek only to point out", he wrote

that the principle of accumulation *based on inequality* was a vital part of the pre-war order of society and of progress as we then understood it, and to emphasise that this principle depended on *unstable psychological conditions*,[33] which it may be impossible to re-create. It was not natural for a population, of whom so few enjoyed the comforts of life, to accumulate so hugely. The war has disclosed the possibility of consumption to all and the vanity of abstinence to many. *Thus the bluff is discovered*; the labouring classes may be no longer willing to forgo so largely, and the capitalist classes, no longer confident of the future, may seek to enjoy more fully their liberties of consumption so long as they last, and thus precipitate the hour of their confiscation.[34]

It was not the unnaturalness for a population to accumulate which brought to Europe the economic chaos at the time Keynes was writing. It was not the discovery of a bluff. It was due to political defeat which brought with it economic and monetary disorder. The resulting inflation undermined – as it is undermining now – the possibility of long-term, meaningful, monetary arrangements. Economic rewards were no longer related to individual expectations but to speculative gains or losses from the depreciation of money. Indeed, Keynes himself portrayed, in a description which has become historic, the nature, significance and effects of inflation.[35]

Moreover, he described the weakness and malpractices of Governments which had brought Europe to this pass. He pointed out that those very same Governments sought "to direct on to a class known as 'profiteers' the popular indignation against the more obvious consequences of their vicious methods." They did this knowing full well that they were attacking "the active and constructive element in the whole capitalist society"; that, in a period of rapidly rising prices, the profits were the consequence and not a cause of rising prices. "By combining a popular hatred of the class of entrepreneurs with the blow already given to social security by the violent and arbitrary disturbance of contract and of the established equilibrium of wealth which is the inevitable result of inflation, these governments are fast rendering impossible a continuance of the social and economic order of the nineteenth century. But they have no plan for replacing it".[36]

But one might well ask, should not "public wisdom" have guided Governments to prevent all this? According to Keynes, however, failure was allegedly due to the capitalist class itself. How did this occur? Because, in his opinion, Europe was faced with an extraordinary weakness on the part of the great capitalist class. In the nineteenth century the capitalists believed in themselves and their value to society. They thought it proper to continue in the full enjoyment of their riches and power. But now they allowed themselves to be ruined and undone by Governments of their own making and by a Press which they owned. So Keynes made it appear as if the monetary order was a class order: the owners of capital, as investors, as landlords, or as "an order of society" were to be regarded as responsible for their own destruction. "No order of society", he wrote, "ever perishes save by its own hand."[37]

What an odd explanation! Indeed, one might well ask why it should be relevant now? The answer is that it reflects consciously or unconsciously that ambivalence to the monetary economy which, in an even more extreme form, characterizes many of our present attitudes. On the one hand, keynes appreciated to the full the beneficence and efficiency of the monetary economy. On the other hand, he saw it falling apart and could not account for its doing so. He fell into the very error which he condemned – the error of personifying alleged causes. He projected on to the capitalists the final responsibility for failing to prevent Governments from making scapegoats of them. Simmel also was, as we have seen, concerned about the effects of a monetary economy – but he did not fall into this kind of rationalizing. He had a very different and more objective view of the interrelations involved in society's functioning.

A Simple Hypothesis

In any case there is so far no evidence that it is owing to the actions of the owners of capital, as lenders or financiers, that the occurrence of booms and depressions, of inflation or deflation is really due. In a dignified tribute to Keynes, Friedman states that at the heart of the General Theory lies an extremely simple hypothesis:[38] "A new, bold, and imaginative hypothesis, whose virtue was precisely how much it could say *about major problems on the basis of so little*.[39] Of course, his assumptions were not in literal correspondence with reality. If they had been, he would have been condemned to pedestrian description; his whole theory would have lost its power. Of course, he could be wrong." Indeed, he argued that there is no point to any scientific theory that cannot be wrong: The greater the range of evidence that, if observed, would contradict a theory, the more precise are its predictions and the better a theory, "*provided it is not, in fact, contradicted*".

Friedman believed that Keynes's theory was the right kind of theory in its simplicity, its concentration on a few key magnitudes and its potential fruitfulness. He rejected it, not on these grounds, but because he thought that it had been contradicted by evidence. Its predictions had not been confirmed by experience. This failure, he wrote, "suggests that it has not isolated what are 'really' the key factors in short-run economic change".

Deceit in Monetary Policy

But if Friedman's criticism is correct, his belief that Keynes was engaged merely in finding a simple fruitful hypothesis does not get to the root of the matter.

This is because Keynes was involved – and the Neo-Keynesians are no less so - in a particular moral issue. No one has to this day been able to escape the consequences of the fact that both he and his successors ignored it. That moral issue is whether it is defensible deliberately to use *public deceit* in *monetary* policy.

Keynes himself gave a clue to his view as early as 1922. As noted by Elizabeth Johnson, while he was writing of Lloyd George's political craft "with introspection into his own personality clearly in mind", he used the phrase "A preference for truth or for sincerity *as a method* may be a prejudice based on some aesthetic or personal standard, inconsistent in politics, with practical good."[40]

Friedman suggests that the Keynesian model is characterized by its simplicity. Its application in practical affairs, in my view, rests on a morality which is even simpler: the morality of initiating monetary policies the consequences of which will appear to others to be different from what they are known or expected to be to those responsible for them.

The essence of the Keynesian prescription is to change the value of money, in the "short period", in order to change (mostly in practice to reduce) the real wage rate – *while appearing to do nothing of the kind*. So also with changes affecting the "burden" of debt.

"Justice" and "Flexibility"

Keynes, in the *General Theory*, explained why he preferred this "flexible" money policy, as he called it, to a "flexible" wage policy. He wrote:[41]

(i) *Except in a socialised community where wage-policy is settled by decree*, there is no means of securing *uniform* wage reductions for every class of labour. The result can only be brought about by a series of gradual, irregular changes, justifiable on no criterion of social justice or economic expediency, and probably completed only after wasteful and disastrous struggles, where those in the weakest bargaining position will suffer relatively to the rest. A change in quantity of money, on the other hand, is already within the power of most governments . . . it can only by a *foolish* person who would prefer a flexible wage policy to a flexible money policy, unless he can point to advantages from the former which are not obtainable from the latter. Moreover, other things being equal, *a method which it is comparatively easy to apply* should be deemed preferable to a method which is probably so difficult as to be impracticable. . . .

(ii) If important classes are to have their remuneration fixed in terms of money in any case, *social justice and social expediency* are best served if the remuneration of *all* factors are somewhat inflexible in terms of money. Having regard to the large groups of incomes which are comparatively inflexible in terms of money, it can only be an *unjust* person who would prefer a flexible wage policy to a flexible money policy, unless he can point to advantages from the former which are not obtainable from the latter.

(iii) The method of increasing the quantity of money in terms of wage-units by decreasing the wage-unit increases proportionately the burden of debt; whereas the method of producing the same result by increasing the quantity of money whilst leaving the wage-unit unchanged has the opposite effect. *Having regard to the excessive burden of many types of debt*, it can only be an *inexperienced* person who would prefer the former.[42]

By such alterations in the value of money, the wage-earners, the investors and the entrepreneurs are to be induced to adopt courses of action which, if they could immediately discern the full consequences of the monetary devices which were being used, they would not enter upon. The motives and movements of the economic actors on the stage are to be influenced by simply deflecting the mirror of money so that they may be led to apprehend a *distorted* image of reality.

At this point, after nearly forty years of debate about whether and how Keynes's key relationships of the rate of interest, investment consumption and saving function, it is salutary to recall his own final assessment of it all. "For my own part", he wrote, in the *General Theory*, in 1935,[43] "I am now somewhat sceptical of the success of a merely *monetary* policy directed towards influencing the rate of interest. I expect to see the *State*, which is in a position to *calculate* the marginal efficiency of capital-goods on long views and on the basis of the general social advantage, taking an ever greater responsibility for directly organising investment; since it seems likely that the fluctuations in the market estimation of the marginal efficiency of different types of capital, . . . will be too great to be offset by any practicable changes in the rate of interest."

As William Breit and Roger L. Ransom have reminded us, Keynes "was himself aware of the appeal of his policy recommendations to totalitarian regimes".[44] They were referring to the preface of the German edition of the *General Theory* in which Keynes wrote:

Nevertheless *the theory of output as a whole, which is what the following book purports to provide, is much more easily adapted to the conditions of a totalitarian state, than is the theory of the production and distribution of a given output produced under conditions of free competition and a large measure of laissez-faire. The theory of the psychological laws* relating consumption and saving, the influence of loan expenditure on prices and real wages, the part played by the rate of interest – these *remain as necessary ingredients in our scheme of thought."*[45]

Money and Morality

There were even deeper drives below the surface which accounted for the direction of Keynes's psychological "laws". Let us take, for example, what he called "the love of money".[46] He wrote:

If there is no *moral* objective in economic progress, then it follows that we must not sacrifice, even for a day, moral to material advantage – in other words, that we may no longer keep business and religion in separate compartments of the soul. In so far as a man's thoughts are capable of straying along these paths, he will be ready to search with curiosity for something at the heart of Communism quite different from the picture of its outward parts which our press paints.

What Keynes had in mind was what he regarded as the moral problem of our age. This was concerned with the *love of money*, with the habitual appeal to the money motive, with the universal striving after *individual economic security*, with the social approbation of *money as the measure of constructive success* and with the *social appeal to the hoarding instinct as the foundation* of the necessary provision for the family and for the future.[47] That is why he thought a revolution in our ways of thinking and feeling about money might be required and that Russian Communism might represent the first confused stirrings of a great religion.[48] He concluded, "Something – there is just a chance – might come out. And even a chance gives to what is happening in Russia more importance than what is happening (let us say) in the United States of America" (p. 270).

One is tempted to consider just exactly what is meant by such a seemingly innocuous phrase as "even a chance gives to what is happening in Russia more importance than what is happening in the United States of America". How is such a chance to be measured or evaluated? Would, for example, the millions who died of starvation or who were purged by Stalin to give Russia "her chance" have been regarded by Keynes as a measure of the cost? Or should the fact that after fifty years Russia has not yet been able to organize her agriculture effectively mean that she had her "chance" but has not yet been able to make use of it?

Keynes thought that, in exalting the common man, communism was but following other famous religions. In this there was nothing new. However, in his view, there was another factor which, in a changed form and a new setting, might contribute something to the true religion of the future. He wrote:

Leninism is absolutely, defiantly non-supernatural, and its emotional and ethical essence centres about the individual's and the community's attitude towards the love of money[49] . . . I mean that (Russian Communism) tries to construct a framework of society in which pecuniary motives as influencing action shall have a changed relative importance, in which social approbations shall be differently distributed, and where behaviour, which previously was normal and respectable, ceases to be either the one or the other.

The Distrust of Money

These are not isolated instances of Keynes's genius for reflecting the deep-seated emotions of society. The sensitivity of his antennae in this regard is shown by the remark that: "In Europe – or at least in some parts of Europe – but not, I think in the United States of America – there is a latent reaction, somewhat widespread, against basing society to the extent that we do upon fostering, encouraging, and protecting the money-motives of individuals." And he added, "A preference for arranging our affairs in such a way as to appeal to the money-motive as little as possible, rather than as much as possible, need not be entirely *a priori* but may be based on the comparison of experiences."[50]

But his own distrust of the *money-motive* goes even further. As Dudley Dillard[51] has pointed out, Keynes was primarily concerned with the Theory of a Monetary Economy. The evils he wished to correct were regarded by him as arising out of the very fact that we were living in a money economy. This even caused him to consider whether abolition of money would be possible. In the *Festschrift für Arthur Spiethoff*[52] Keynes expressed the view that the main reason why the Problem of Crises remained unsolved lay in the lack of what might be termed a Monetary Theory of Production. He developed this theme in terms of a distinction between Monetary Economics and Real-Exchange Economics. The former he defined as one in which Money played a part of its own and affected motives and decisions. Therefore, the course of events could not be predicted without a knowledge of the behaviour of money.

It was in order to "take away the preferred position in the hierarchy of wealth"[53] that Keynes was fascinated by mechanistic nostrums, like Gesell's proposal for stamped-money. He wanted, thereby, to increase the carrying costs on money so as to make it more like other assets. Dillard rightly drew attention to the fact that "While Keynes avoids most of the pitfalls of utopian monetary reformers, like Robert Owen, John Gray, John Francis Bray, Proudhon and Silvio Gesell, his thought has much in common with theirs."

All reject Say's law of markets because of its neutral money implications; all view interest as a monetary phenomenon; all are vigorously opposed to the gold standard; all are anti-rentier and pro-entrepreneur; all adhere to or are sympathetic to the labour theory of value; and they distinguish the financial and industrial sphere of capitalism, blaming the former for unemployment and other economic ills, while finding no major fault with industrial circulation. The purpose of their monetary reforms was an economic environment in which supply would create its own demand. But Keynes was far too intelligent to believe that money could be got rid of so easily. He realized that we could not get rid of money, even by abolishing gold and silver and legal-tender instruments, so long as there existed any durable asset capable of possessing monetary attributes.[54] The way out would be to see to it that there were no such assets, i.e. to go the whole hog and to destroy the free monetary order and the exchange economy, as was done in communist societies.

Keynes, however, first sought a different solution: to use money itself as a means of escape from the alleged evils of a monetary economy.He was aware of the dangers along this route. Many of his followers were not. The dangers were due to the fact that "money itself rapidly loses the attribute of liquidity if its future supply is expected to undergo sharp changes"[55] – i.e. that it will be rejected!

The Belief in Public Wisdom

What he advocated was to use the monetary order, by means of what he called "public wisdom", to influence the business man "steeped in the narrow arts of commercial calculation", whom he accused of not being able to calculate from a social point of view. Referring to the well-known picture of the great Captain of Industry, the Master-Individualist, who serves us in serving himself, just as any other artist does,[56] he wrote: "Yet this one, in his turn, is becoming a tarnished idol. We grow more doubtful whether it is he who will lead us into paradise by the hand."

Keynes's overall view is summed up in the statement:

. . . more often individuals acting separately to promote their own ends are too ignorant or too weak to attain even these. Experience does *not* show that individuals, when they make up a social unit, are always less clear-sighted than when they act separately. [From this he concluded]: We cannot therefore settle on abstract grounds, but must handle on its merits in detail what Burke termed[57] "one of the finest problems in legislation, namely, to determine what the State ought to take upon itself to direct by the public wisdom, and what it ought to leave, with as little interference as possible, to individual exertion".[58]

This view, however reasonable it looks at first sight, is really based on a mistaken assumption: that public wisdom is something apart from or outside private wisdom. But wisdom – that rare commodity – is never "public". It is always incorporated in individual action as *permitted* by law and custom or as violating them. Moreover, in the course of the long debate on *laissez-faire*, it was never implied that all individuals either should or could act wisely. It was held that it is the interaction of relative wisdom and relative ignorance by *different* individuals which finally leads to decisions and actions, in the market, which are likely – by cancelling out individual errors – to best meet Society's need to adapt to changing situations. To condemn the money-motive, as Keynes repeatedly did, overlooks that the pursuit of the money-motive is nothing but the pursuit of the *purposes* which it is believed can be attained through money. It is not the love of money as such but the love of things or services for which money can be used that normally constitutes the *motive* of individual action. By regarding the money-motive as the villain of the piece, Keynes made respectable the deliberate creation, by the State, of Money Illusion to influence saving, investment and the rate of interest: thereby to overcome the alleged inefficiency and ignorance of individuals. The fact is that the deliberate creation of Money Illusion is a form of social deceit. If persisted in, it must, finally, subvert the monetary order.

It does this for two reasons. The first is technical and, in a free society, inevitable: it is because, once the "bluff has been discovered", to use Keynes's own words,[59] individuals will soon take countervailing action. Of this, in the form of increased wage demands and other price adjustments which even anticipate the expected rate of inflation, no one needs at present to be reminded. The second is less obvious but more fundamental. It is because to use the monetary system as a means of creating illusions concerning the future in order thereby to influence individual intentions and actions, in accordance with the beliefs of those who propagate them, is to destroy the *moral* authority of the monetary order. As John Rawls[60] has put it, "certain ways of dealing with envy and other aberrant propensities are closed to a well-ordered society. For example, it cannot keep them in check by promulgating false or unfounded beliefs."

To give the impression that the value of money will not be adversely affected by particular policies, which those responsible for them well know will be the case, is to deliberately propagate a false belief. But, as we have seen, without trust a free monetary order loses the foundation on which it can alone be built.

What then, one must ask, accounts for the role which Keynes assigned to money at the risk – of which he was fully aware – of destroying the free monetary economy. Once again we find that he had his own psychological theories and fears about individual human behaviour but little if any evidence to support them. In one form or another, they influenced his outlook on monetary policies and still continue to shape our own.

Speculative and "Real" Investment

Keynes had an almost obsessive fear that speculation or gambling would predominate over investment based on "the best genuine long-term expectations". However he did admit that there were serious-minded individuals and that it made a vast difference to an investment market whether or not they predominated in their influence over the game-players.[61] But he thought investment based on genuine long-term expectations to be so difficult today as to be scarcely practicable. It involved greater risks than trying to guess better than the crowd how the crowd would behave; and, given equal intelligence, the making of more disastrous mistakes. There was no clear evidence from experience that the investment policy which was socially advantageous coincided with that which was most profitable. It needed more intelligence to defeat the forces of time and our ignorance of the future than to beat the gun. Life was not long enough. Human nature desired quick results: there was a peculiar zest in making money quickly, and remoter gains were discounted by the average man at a very high rate. The game of professional investment appeared to him to be intolerably boring and over-exacting to anyone who was entirely exempt from the gambling instinct; whilst he who had it had to pay to this propensity the appropriate toll.

No facts were adduced by Keynes as to the relative size of "speculative and real" investment decisions – if indeed, which I doubt, the distinction is meaningful. It is also doubtful whether the distinction between long-term and near-term investment is as significant as Keynes suggested. In market-oriented activity in a money economy the short-term shades into the long-term as far as bearing or hedging against risk is concerned. The whole process of investment is, as I have shown elsewhere,[62] much more like "laying off" long-term bets by replacing them by short-term ones as the day of the race draws nearer. It is a matter of being able to shift the burden of risk on to the shoulders most able and willing to bear it. The long-term investor or entrepreneur cannot afford to ignore near-term market fluctuations: on the contrary, he has of necessity to take account of those that are relevant: he has to acquire (or dispose of) such assets as are now more (or less) suitable to his on-going investment strategy than was the case when they were first acquired.

Keynes did not view the matter in this light. The spectacle of modern investment markets at times moved him to conclude that it might be useful to make the purchase of an investment permanent and indissoluble, like marriage. This would force the investor to direct his mind to the long-term prospects and to those only. But there was a dilemma because the fact that each individual investor flatters himself that his commitment is "liquid" (though this cannot be true for all investors collectively) "calms his nerves and makes him much more willing to take a risk".[63] In my opinion, this is an unfortunate analogy. The investor's belief in short-term liquidity is not illusory, any more than it is illusory for people to believe that their bank deposits are liquid. For under normal circumstances people do not all run to their bank to withdraw their deposits collectively. There are usually no grounds for them to believe that this will occur. Similarly investors have normally no reason to endeavour, or to assume that others will endeavour, to liquidate their investments collectively.[64]

Keynes's remedy is worse than the disease. He suggested abolishing the situation in which "it is open to the individual to employ his wealth in hoarding or lending *money*",[65] by once more calling upon that *deus ex machina*,[66] the State. The latter, he thought, "is in a position to calculate the marginal efficiency of capital-goods on *long* views and on the basis of the *general social advantage*, taking on ever greater responsibility for *directly* organising investment"! Since individuals could not be trusted to make the "right" decisions for the future or undertake the "right" risks, he concluded: "The only radical cure for the crises of confidence which afflict the economic life of the modern world would be *to allow the individual no choice* between consuming his income and ordering the production of the specific capital-assets which, even though it be on precarious evidence, impresses him as the most promising investment available to him."[67] But when in 1923 he had written a shortened version of the first chapter of *A Tract on Monetary Reform*,[68] he was much concerned about the effect of monetary policy on the confidence of investors. "If we are to continue to draw the voluntary savings of the community into 'investments'," he wrote, "we must make it a prime object of deliberate state policy that the standard of value in terms of which they are expressed, should be kept stable." Later this was *replaced by doubts concerning individual decision-making.*[69] He then expressed the view that economic prosperity was excessively dependent on a political and social atmosphere which was congenial to the average business man.[70] In estimating the prospects of investment, we should have regard, therefore, to the nerves and hysteria and even the digestions and reactions to the weather of those upon whose spontaneous activity it largely depended.

The Monetary System as "Illusion"

Once again we find ourselves face to face with the basic Keynesian diagnosis. True to the spirit of his time it associates the failure of the businessman and the entrepreneur with *money motivations and money calculations*. These, it is alleged, are inadequate because they are not *scientific* and they are not scientific because they are based on wealth[71] (i.e. *money-getting motives*) which are in his view incapable of dealing with uncertainty. This is because "about these matters there is no *scientific* basis on which to form any calculable probability whatever. *We simply do not know*. Nevertheless, the necessity for action and for decision compels us as practical men to do our best to overlook this awkward fact and to behave exactly as we should if we had behind us a good *Benthamite calculation* of a series of prospective advantages and disadvantages, each multiplied by its appropriate probability, waiting to be summed"[72] (p. 214).

The contrast with Simmel's philosophy of money could not be more striking. For Keynes, the whole monetary system is in the last resort a kind of illusion, "a contrived system of pretty, polite techniques, *made for a well-panelled board room and a nicely regulated market*[73] – to lull the capitalist, the business man, the entrepreneur into the practice of calmness and immobility, of certainty and security." But these contrivances are liable to collapse. Vague panic fears and unreasoned hopes are not really lulled. They lie but a little way below the surface. And why is this so? It is because *"knowing that our own individual judgement is worthless* we endeavour to fall back on the judgement of the rest of the world, which is perhaps better informed". To make the point quite clear he stressed that we endeavour to conform with the behaviour of the majority or the average. Each individual is endeavouring to copy the others. This leads to what he calls a *conventional judgement*. If this were true the Battle of Britain would never have been fought. Churchill, and everyone else, would simply have calculated the probabilities of success or of failure and have given in to Hitler without batting an eyelid.

No amount of calculation can make the unknowable knowable. Moreover, if it were true that we generally assume the existing state of opinion, there would be no innovations, no change in tastes, choices or techniques, nor any differences in judgement about the meaning of present or past events. It is precisely because of different individual interpretations of these that the pushes and pulls of the market come into being and bring about the continual price changes in which they express themselves.

In contrast to Keynesian and much present-day thinking, for Simmel, and his contemporaries, the monetary system was not one which had been *contrived* to lull individuals into a false sense of security. For them, as I have shown, it represented social interaction and mutual trust in the face of and as a means of combating insecurity, uncertainty and ignorance. For them it reflects the ability of individuals to assert their freedom of choice through individual experimentation, and innovative action, the results of which are subject to acceptance or rejection through the market. It reflects an *open* system of action precisely because it denies that knowledge of what has to be done in the face of uncertainty is *given* to anyone, however wise: it has continually, incessantly, and of necessity, to be discovered afresh in every society subject to change.

I conclude this chapter by suggesting that the answer to the question I raised earlier (as to what Keynes was trying to escape from) is: from the Monetary Economy itself. But even if he escaped from this dilemma of his own creation his successors remain in confused debate. The confusion arises from his assertion that the problems of a monetary economy are essentially different from other economies because of our ignorance of and uncertainty about the future. But why should one believe or imply that the problems of life – for that is what ignorance and uncertainty in the face of fate amount to – should be ascribed to money or be solved by the mechanics of monetary management? The dilemma which Keynes presented is false. It is because we still feel ourselves to be trapped by it that we have to examine it further.

The dilemma arises out of a category mistake similar to that we have previously encountered. It results from regarding a money economy as essentially different from a presumed real-exchange economy.

Keynes, as we have seen, thought of a real-exchange economy as one in which money did not enter into "motives and decisions". In a money economy, by contrast, he thought "money plays a part of its own" and affects motives and decisions. Keynes criticized the classical and neo-classical economists, such as Marshall and Pigou, because, as he put it, in their view, though money is made use of for convenience, it may be considered "to *cancel* out"[74] for most purposes. This is a misleading criticism. Money does not cancel out anything – only goods and services can do that. Even in the purest form of real-exchange economy there will always be transactions which do *not* cancel out. There will be promises, obligations and expectations, and there will be promises unkept and expectations unfulfilled – falsified by events, by ignorance or by deceit. It is not the entry of money upon the scene which gives rise to these imbalances. The "motives and decisions" of people are not altered through the presence or absence of money. This was, as we have seen, why Simmel, in my view so rightly, drew an analogy between abstract concepts of money and abstract concepts like "power" or "reason".

Motives arising from greed, envy, hate, selfishness or from love and altruism are not due to money, nor are stubbornness or amenability to compromise. It is not the money-economy which makes men either flexible or inflexible in their wage-bargaining: it is their bargaining power or the political power they can enlist to reinforce it.

Moreover, uncertainty, about which Keynes was so concerned, exists in all societies. There is no proof that it is increased in a money economy, anymore than there is reason to believe that it is increased through the development of man's reason, or the abstract concepts in which it may sometimes be expressed. Even "hoarding" in the face of uncertainty – as Keynes stressed when he pointed out that almost any form of wealth can be used for the purpose – is a symptom of fear or ignorance of what should be done next. But such fear is not specific to, or especially characteristic of, a monetary economy. Even non-monetary "underdeveloped" economies are subject to the same inability to secure "full employment" due to ignorance of what to do, or fear of the risks involved, with the result that they suffer "stagnation" as severe, and often much more so, as that in any sophisticated money economy. Ignorance and indecisiveness whether under free enterprise or socialist planning, are not monetary phenomena.

The category mistake which I have been discussing is one to which others besides Keynes have fallen victim. Keynes's demand for a new moral order to take the place of the Monetary Economy, in which, according to him, the narrow calculating interests of the business man predominate, is a view of "rational" action which has much in common with the view of Max Weber. The latter went so far as to maintain that such rational decisions as made by business can only be regarded as "rational" in a purely formal sense. He maintained that decisions based on the methods of calculation which happen to be technically available were insufficient: The ultimate ends pursued by society had to be taken into account. Completely rational action was only that which was based on what he called "substantive rationality". The latter had to be interpreted in terms of a set of ultimate values – no matter what they might be[75] – religious, political or aesthetic. What Weber meant was that purely formal rationality, such as in business accounting or management, could be attained only at the expense of *conflict* with other important ideas of value or welfare. For him the business order and similar "technical" structures were, in the last resort, substantively *irrational*.

David Beetham has recently[76] suggested that in fact the concept of *formal rationality*

becomes by default the sole consideration in *Economy and Society*. The calculability of economic processes becomes the standard in terms of which everything is assessed. Thus the expropriation of the workers is presented as a means to improved calculability, their traditionalist attitudes become so many "hindrances" to rationality. For the workers to have a say in management produces all kinds of "technically irrational obstacles and economic irrationalities", whereas, on the other hand, to adjust their psycho-physical apparatus in every detail to the machine represents the "supreme triumph" of scientific management. The concern is to know what are the "conditions for the maximum calculability of labour productivity"; what the conditions for the "maximum rationality of capital accounting". Technical calculability becomes here both the standard of achievement and the criterion for defining what is problematic. Because any substantive position would involve a value judgement, technical rationality is left holding the field; it becomes the definitive standpoint from which everything is assessed.[77]

In my opinion this criticism makes confusion worse confounded. The category mistake that both Keynes and Weber made, and which their followers make today, is to suggest that to express the goals of society or to calculate them in terms of money is one thing, whereas goals or values which cannot be so measured or expressed are another: that there is a real or ultimate rationality which necessarily transcends the pursuit of goals expressed in money terms.

This view, in my opinion, is fallacious. It involves an infinite regress[78] of rationalities or of values which are designated as "substantively rational". Keynes, as I noted earlier, called for a "moral" revolution in order to make possible the pursuit of "ultimate" goals. He then suggested that communism might have something more to offer than the ideal displayed in societies which make use of the money calculus. But, as I have shown, the money-oriented activities of society are just a part of its activities. Like any other part, they can be expanded or circumscribed. But to speak as if decisions in money terms or social actions based on money calculations are less "rational" than other decisions is to make a category mistake. The point, I wish to stress again, is that in an economy, where certain activities or goals are expressed in terms of the calculus of money, society has already thereby chosen the form its activities are to take. It is not as if society consisted of two parts one of which thinks and acts in terms of money and another in terms of non-money. There is a parallel here with Ryle's analogy, to which I referred in Chapter I. In regard to this I expressed the view:[79]

that when, by using a common unit of account, we add up "net values" of certain events or happenings (goods and services) we are simply "measuring" certain parts of a larger whole. . . . Similarly, when we say that we have measured the increase in the value of goods and services produced in a society, we cannot then proceed to speak about this increase causing a *further* increase in the welfare (or "ecfare") of society. An increase in the amount of goods and services does not affect the total welfare of society, except *by definition* through this very increase or decrease in such goods and services themselves. . . .

A society which glorifies war will have a different "system or concept of welfare" . . . from one which desires peace. It is said of the Bushmen of South Africa that no attempts to bring them to adopt the social life of a modern community were at any time successful. They remained hunters – notwithstanding their high intelligence, capability of practising arable agriculture and of creating other goods and services – because they liked hunting. Hunting was their ideal form of welfare and, therefore, "income" to the Bushmen (if we can use the word in this context at all) was defined in terms of success in the chase and in the substance yielded by the chase alone. Such "income" could not be compared with "equivalent" goods and services which might have resulted from some other form of activity, or with "income" in a society of non-hunters.

A monetary economy depends on a vast number of circumstances arising out of the history, mores, beliefs and political and economic experience of society as a whole. It cannot be separated from them. That is why a dependable and free monetary order is a relatively rare phenomenon in the history of nations. It can be easily misunderstood, as we shall see in the next chapter.

CHAPTER VI

Freedom and Monetary Order

There is a hope, and it is this: having become so impressed with the fact that freedom is not everything or the only thing, perhaps we shall put that discovery behind us and comprehend, before it is too late, that without freedom all else is nothing. G. Warren Nutter.[1]

Contrasting Philosophies

If one wished to characterize the present monetary situation of the free world in one word, that word would be "mistrust". Not since 1914 has it been so general. Not a single currency is completely untouched by apprehension and suspicion. Not one country now enjoys the confidence which the money of the main European countries commanded before the First World War. After it, an internationally recognized expert could confidently write a book called *The Restoration of the World's Currencies*.[2] Nobody would use such an optimistic title nowadays.

It is my contention that the current world monetary mistrust is due not only to an ambivalent attitude to money but reflects also a deliberate attack on the monetary economy. It arises out of the conflict between money as a *tool* of state action and money as a symbol of social trust. The two conceptions are incompatible. I go so far as to contend that for several decades we have been witnessing an intense re-action against traditional concepts of the monetary order: it is not far removed from a revolt against it.

I have attempted to illustrate the basic ideas responsible for this situation by discussing two contrasting philosophies of money. Both philosophies are pessimistic – but for very different reasons. It is important to try to understand these differences. Simmel, for example, was pessimistic about the possibility of the survival of *any* free monetary order. This is because his thinking was inspired, not by the question what the State or the Government or individuals were able to do *with* money, but by the question what abstract conceptions of money were doing to them: more specifically, what these were doing to the mutual trust and confidence on which the continuance of free individual interrelations in society depended.

He was pessimistic because he saw an inherent tendency for the progressive development of an advanced money economy to lead to its own destruction. He did not have in mind merely the *mechanical* failure of the monetary system; although he frequently warned against the shatteringly destructive effects of inflation. Unlike Keynes, he was also not prepared to ascribe the failure to a set of psychological re-actions or behaviouristic patterns which could be designated arbitrarily as "right" or "wrong", "inert" or "flexible", "stubborn" or "enlightened" and linked to the reactions and decisions of wage-earners, entrepreneurs, creditors, debtors, consumers, producers or any other particular *class* of persons one might care to name and blame and – by monetary manipulation – bring to heel or stimulate to move.

Simmel's doubts went much deeper: they can be summarized in the form of two other questions.

First, whether people would continue to accept the increasingly abstract ways of thinking involved in the growing complexity of monetary relations.

Second, whether the abstractions, in which monetary relations are necessarily increasingly expressed, would not give rise to serious misconceptions concerning the unlimited power of money itself and lead to the ultimate destruction of the free monetary order.

It is clear that these doubts are the obverse and reverse of the same coin. On the one side, they characterize the feeling of helplessness of the individual over against what appear to him as the inscrutable powers of money. On the other side, they express the feeling that the mere possession of money confers on the owner infinite, god-like power itself.

The first of these conceptions leads to alienation from money; the second to over-estimation of what the possessor, be he an individual, a company, a corporation or the state, can do with it. Both conceptions lead eventually to a revolt against it. On the one hand, alienation from money leads to dissatisfaction with life within the money economy which appears incomprehensible and burdensome to an increasing number of individuals. On the other hand, over-estimation of the powers of money has similar consequences to those of the over-estimation of the power of abstract reason which eventually leads to a violent reaction against it and to its rejection when the projections of its powers fail.[3]

The ever-increasing demand for direct government action to replace the market economy illustrates the over-estimation both of the power of abstract reason (as public "wisdom") and of the power of abstract money. It rests on the belief that both can bring about the achievement of any and every set of goals. When the goals are not reached the initial response to the failure is always the same: "Apply more reason" or more "money".

I am reminded of a rebellion in German East Africa – known as the "MAJI–MAJI" ("water – water") rebellion – when the witch-doctors assured the rebels against German rule that smearing their bodies with a kind of "holy" water would protect them. After wave upon wave had been mown down by the bullets of government troops, the African soldiers complained to their witch-doctors that the "holy" water was ineffective: the latter replied, "Don't despair, you have obviously not applied enough water (MAJI), put on more and do not be afraid!"

Reason and Money

In the over-estimation of the powers both of reason and of money the error is always the same. It consists in over-looking that in practical affairs both reason and money, considered in the abstract, are only like rules of formal behaviour. In themselves they are devoid of specific content. They have to be applied to meet each different event or problem as it arises.

So blinding are the imagined powers of abstract money that they even lead to attempts to obtain them at the expense of others. Simmel, indeed, thought that the long resentment of the Church against money rested on the belief in its limitless powers. Money, therefore, came to be regarded by the Church as likely to lead to an unfortunate confusion, resting on a too close parallel between the formlessness and abstraction of the highest economic and the highest cosmic unity.

Religious bodies therefore frequently attempted to dethrone the powers of money in the eyes of men. Similarly, the socialist desire to abolish the free money economy is in part based on the belief that the power of money should be reserved for the State, whose goals must not be exposed to competition from the money-power of free individuals or other organizations.

What all such beliefs overlook is that the powers of money are always only potential. They have to be translated – into specific but previously unknown and undisclosed actions. They always rest ultimately on a body of rules and practices to which society adheres. "*Man*", as Professor Peters has so aptly expressed it, "*is a rule-following animal*. His actions are not simply directed towards ends; they also conform to social standards and conventions, and unlike a calculating machine he acts because of his knowledge of rules and objectives".[4]

The Monetary Order as Tool or Rule

The basic difference between the two philosophies of money which I have been considering is that the one endeavours to incorporate the view that the monetary system should be regarded as a means for the achievement of specific and immediate goals of public policy, while the other regards this view as incompatible with a monetary order: the pursuit of changing goals of action will make it capricious and uncertain and prey to conflicting and varying political objectives. The view that the monetary order should be used as a tool of political or social action is in part analogous to that which has been described by Richard R. Brandt[5] as a form of "act-utilitarianism" in opposition to one he describes as "rule-utilitarianism". His analysis is apparently based on a "material conception of morality"[6] with the truth of which I am not here concerned. He calls a utilitarianism "act-utilitarianism"

if it holds that the rightness of an act is fixed by the utility of *its* consequences, as compared with those of other acts the agent might perform instead. Act-utilitarianism is hence an atomistic theory: the value of the effects of a single act on the world is decisive for its rightness. "Rule-utilitarianism," in contrast, applies to views according to which the rightness of an act is not fixed by *its* relative utility, but by conformity with general rules or principles; the utilitarian feature of these theories consists in the fact that the correctness of these rules or principles is fixed in some way by the utility of their general acceptance. In contrast with the atomism of act-utilitarianism, rule-utilitarianism is in a sense an organic theory: the rightness of individual acts can be ascertained only by assessing a whole social policy. (Ibid, p. 109)

Before I proceed, let me stress that I do not here enter into the discussion of the view whether it is possible (which I doubt) to assess a whole social policy or the "rightness of individual acts in relation thereto". What I am concerned with is the *implication* of "act-utilitarianism" which as Brandt points out "it is difficult to accept". He illustrates why this is so by the following:

It implies that if you have employed a boy to mow your lawn and he has finished the job and asks for his pay, you should pay him what you promised only if you cannot find a better use for your money. It implies that when you bring home your monthly pay-check you should use it to support your family and yourself only if it cannot be used more effectively to supply the needs of others. It implies that if your father is ill and has no prospect of good in his life, and maintaining him is a drain on the energy and enjoyments of others, then, if you can end his life without provoking any public scandal or setting a bad example, it is your positive duty to take matters into your own hands and bring his life to a close. A virtue of rule-utilitarianism, in at least some of its forms is that it avoids at least some of such objectionable implications. (Ibid, p. 109)

In the case of a free monetary order examples of the danger of actions analogous to "act-utilitarianism" are, as we have seen, not difficult to find.

"My Fellow Americans"

The element of the absurd in the claims now made by national states in relation to money has been high-lighted by Mr. Art Buchwald, one of the leading columnists of our time.

The humorous columnist today plays the same role as the fool does in Shakespeare's plays when he holds up to kings the mirror in which their follies are reflected. Art Buchwald holds up to the American democracy the mirror in which the absurdity of some of its ways are made visible. The scenario in Buchwald's piece "My Fellow Americans" is Mr. Nixon addressing the American people to reveal what the Administration proposes to do about food prices, which, it was claimed by one of his advisers, were the main remaining cause of inflation.

So Mr. Buchwald constructs Mr. Nixon's speech as follows:

My Fellow Americans,
I have asked to speak to you tonight on a subject that is vital to everyone in this country. When I took office three and a half years ago, this country was on the road to inflation; an inflation that touched every household, every man, woman and child in this great land of ours. I vowed at the time to do something about it and I am happy to report to you tonight that my efforts have succeeded. I can now tell you that the price of baseball cards is down 8 per cent, the cost of trolley-car tracks has been reduced 0·9 per cent, men's straw hats are selling at one-third the price of 10 years ago. . . . The reason for the success of my anti-inflation program is the willingness of the American people to make sacrifices to stem the tide. . . . Now I know you are going to say. "If the price of food goes up how can we ever hope to hold down inflation?" . . . Ladies and gentlemen, we can lick the problem of the high cost of food if we make one more slight sacrifice. I am asking every person in the nation regardless of race, regardless of age, regardless of party affiliation to stop eating. . . . My fellow Americans, when you go to bed hungry tonight, remember you are not going to bed hungry because there is no food to eat, but you are going to bed hungry because you believe, as I do, in a healthy, stable economy. I don't think I'm exaggerating when I say that if every American gives up eating until the inflation crisis is over, this could go down as the week that changed the history of the world.[7]

The element of the absurd in this parody consists, firstly, in the President blaming the people for the failure of the Administration: that is, of course, what every representative learns to do immediately he is elected. Secondly, it consists in the notion that the balance between money and goods can be restored in a mechanical manner. It overlooks that money is the means of settling a claim. The claim cannot be settled by not meeting it. That is, as we have seen, merely to abrogate it. But to abrogate it is to *hurt* the claimant. That is why after Pat (Nixon's wife) innocently asked whether "there wasn't another way, besides giving up food?" she received the reply "As President of the United States, I must choose the *hard* way."

But, of course, that was the exact opposite of the truth. The people's belief in money, which they could trust, had just been shattered. They were now going to bed hungry because their legitimate claims had not been met through no fault of their's. The appeal to them to choose the hard way was not only absurd – it was a moral sham.

Uncertainties of the People

The confusion in current monetary debates frequently arises from regarding money in philosophical abstract terms as if it could be considered as being apart from the complex, many-sided social and economic factors in which in reality it is embedded.[8] This results in widespread fears of their effects on the everyday concerns of ordinary people. These do not, and obviously cannot, regard money in terms suited to the discussions and prescriptions of philosopher-kings. "The most fundamental function of institutions is probably to protect the individual from having to make too many choices."[9]

It is, therefore, not surprising that monetary manipulation intended to reduce uncertainty has, by destroying faith in the monetary order, actually increased it. A monetary policy which is directed to shifting goals – as, for example, full employment, economic growth, economic equality or the attempt to satisfy conflicting demands of capital and labour – cannot but vary with the goals adopted.

It is significant that the inflation which has resulted from attempts to meet these conflicting demands has even been regarded by some, like Professor Martin Bronfenbrenner,[10] as providing an escape valve for the excess claims of competing income groups which will keep their income conflicts from directly destroying the capitalist free-enterprise system. He argued that the rising feeling of resentment against owners of businesses is not necessarily linked to any philosophical belief that the share of wages in the national income should be increased. The worker merely wants higher wages when he sees the large profits reported by his company and others like it. Bronfenbrenner even suggested that another 20 to 40 per cent of the property income share might be shifted to wages and salaries without undermining the incentives to manage and invest. But, in my opinion, whether 20 per cent or 40 per cent, or even 80 per cent would be the tolerable figure for the economy is not the real issue: rather it is that a society which tries to satisfy *envy* by monetary manipulation will subvert trust in the monetary order – and, eventually, in a free economic order also. Envy cannot be so assuaged – it will simply be expressed in other ways, and its unhappy gaze fixed on something else. As Schoeck concluded, "even when the ideal egalitarian condition has been attained, and everything that can be communally owned has long since been collectivized, there will always be something left that will be a cause for envy and hence will constitute a danger to the community; mere time-space *existence* as an individual and private person is enough to irritate."[11] The fact remains that all manipulations which result in inflation introduce uncertainties which cause people to run for cover from the vagaries of the monetary order.

The growing chaos in monetary policy at home is paralleled abroad. Never before has so much public ink been spilt to proclaim the need for a new international monetary order and machinery to ensure better national policies. But how this is to be achieved, and to what purpose, has not been made apparent. This is not astonishing: on the international, as on the national domestic scene, those who have the power will determine the goals, not only within but outside national boundaries. Since no goals can be agreed on to please all nations, the trustworthiness of money is likely to be greater abroad than at home.

It is hardly necessary to remind the reader that one of the prime causes of inflation has always been war and the preparation for it or the attempt by one nation to appease another by monetary gifts and transfers.

Indicative of the current schisms in the international monetary order is that gold – once the symbol of monetary trust – is now being sold off, not to stabilize world currencies but to meet the political pressures exerted by particular nations. With the final rejection of gold as even an indirect measure of money, we are left only with the so-called "benign" position of no international standard of deferred payments at all. Money has become a matter of what is euphemistically called "liquidity" instead of certainty – of national convenience instead of national or international trust. It is no longer linked to a discernible social ethic: to a body of custom and law which ensures the reliability of monetary policy and practice. For ordinary people, therefore, safety lies in adherence to the faction, group or organization whose influence on monetary policy appears to provide a haven of refuge – however temporary. They are compelled to seek protection for themselves at the expense of others.

To them, the world of money often appears to resemble a nightmare: in it representatives of many nations are seated around a table. They are playing a game which only they can comprehend. The essence of it appears to be that each player has the right to pay his losses in tokens which he prints as he likes and to receive his winnings from others in tokens which they have printed as they like. Moreover, each of the national representatives can alter the rules of the game as he likes, whenever he so desires. Around the table stand a mass of ordinary people who have to make a living as best they can by using the tokens of their own nation or those of other nations if they can somehow acquire them. All are feverishly disposing of the tokens they happen to have received to exchange them for others which will prove of more lasting value.

An Intellectual Contest?

The language of monetary policy today makes it appear as if nations were engaged in an intellectual contest. Each is imagined to be assessing the costs and benefits of altering its domestic monetary policies to outwit the others.

William Fellner[12] perspicaciously suggested that the current international monetary debates and policies are based on forms of "neo-mercantilist reasoning" which, he reminds us, even Adam Smith called "partly solid and partly sophistical", although probably today the wording of the phrase should be reversed. Fellner is contrasting systems, like Bretton Woods, which had a bias towards fixed exchange rates, with those with greater flexibility. He rightly emphasized that the "sophistical" part of the argument used outside the U.S.A. for keeping dollar-rates fixed rests on the fact that export industries and those producing import-substitutes find it profitable to have their domestic currency undervalued. These industries are powerful in most countries and so are the unions in them. By directing attention to sectoral problems, they somehow get round the fact that it is basically a poor deal to go on receiving for one's exports claims in money (dollars) instead of goods.

I do not wish to discuss here the validity of the arguments for fixed versus flexible exchange rates. I wish to illustrate the hold which abstract and mechanical analogies have on current approaches to these questions. When Fellner suggests that many countries have been uncertain concerning the proper "location" of their currency in a "true" equilibrium structure, allowing for the steps to be taken by other countries, he is under the spell of abstract language. It is just this which has caused the role of power in monetary affairs to be exaggerated by national policy makers. For it is not obvious how they can judge the "proper" location of their currency in the future or ensure that it will be established if they could.

One cannot escape from the fundamental issues involved in monetary order by assuming that there is nothing more to a monetary system than to deal with "problems" or "crises" as they arise – as if, by analogy, a marriage is but an agreement between husband and wife to decide on its purpose afresh every morning, in the light of what happened the day before. The element of the absurd, which we recognize instinctively in this notion, is that the marital state means, if it has any meaning at all, that it continues in spite of, not because of, any immediate or chance circumstance. It is a continuing moral relationship. A completely pragmatic marriage is a contradiction in terms. Marriage reflects the dependable and trustworthy character of the parties: without this it is but a form lacking content.

That is, I believe, what Simmel implies when he says that money in itself has no character. Its character depends on what man in society breathes into it. It can become the instrument of the highest forms of free individual development and cultural achievement. However, it can also be used to destroy all free subjective strivings by collective or authoritarian decisions. It can be the instrument of freedom or of tyranny.

I believe that it is because we have in the past regarded and continue to regard money as possessing a character and power of its own, that we fail to realize the real nature of the current monetary debate. That debate is basically not about inflation or deflation, fixed or flexible exchange rates, gold or paper standards and so forth, it is about the kind of society in which money is to operate.

Public Debts

From whatever angle we approach the problem, we are always brought back to the question of what society really wants the role of money to be and to the schismatic conflicts concerning it. Perhaps nothing is more revealing of them than the new view of public debts and the diminished interest in money's role as a standard of deferred payments or standard of value. As I have shown, there is implicit in the idea of money, as a means of communication, the question "for whom and for what". I believe that it is implicit also in money's function as a standard of deferred payments. Fifty years ago it was still considered of prime importance for the savings and investments on which the highly developed monetary economies of the world were built. It is no longer so considered. It is now the turn of public debtors to be regarded as the lynch-pin of the social and economic order: their obligations are viewed in a very different light than they once were.

A crude symptom of this is the current tendency to blame *creditor* countries for achieving a trading surplus in their balance of payments and to praise debtor countries for the opposite. Everybody knows how absurd this view is. Its very absurdity indicates the underlying psychological conflict. It arises from the unpalatable idea that debt involves a promise of repayment. It is this which is being relegated to the background or suppressed. Consequently the idea of maintaining the value of money suffers the same fate.

The same change in attitude has taken place in relation to transactions between different sectors within countries. Nobody could have foreseen forty years ago the large extent to which the economies of the free world would come to rest on debts incurred by local and central Governments, as a result of due deliberation or forced upon them by sectional or political pressure groups. There has also been a considerable shift in the relative position of debtors and creditors.

Professor G.L. Bach has recently published some significant calculations on both these aspects.[13] They show that the debt owed by Governments, in the United States, grew more than five-fold between 1939 and 1972. There was also a very considerable growth in the monetary debts of business and financial corporations.

The counterpart to all this was a ten-fold increase in the net monetary assets which were held by householders in the form of loans to government and to business and finance. As a result of inflation, there was a massive transfer of wealth to governments. Roughly 1·6 trillion dollars of creditor's claims (i.e. bank deposits, currency, mortgages, bonds and the like) was wiped out by inflation in the U.S.A. between 1946 and 1974 on the assumption that no adjustments were made by creditors to anticipate or compensate for it. But even if it had been anticipated through higher interest rates, Bach suggests that total creditor-debtor transfers from inflation were perhaps one-half to two-thirds of a trillion dollars.[14]

Most other countries have had much larger shifts in creditor–

debtor relations than occurred in the U.S.A., because of the growth in the role of the State and the use of public debt to finance it.

The Moral Issue

The causes and consequences of these changes in the debt structure are complex. I am here concerned only with what is perhaps the most important of all the factors involved. It is the belief that it does not really matter who creates debt as long as it is created; and that the government can always be relied upon to do so. Moreover it can always "repay" it by increasing the money supply. According to this view the creation of public debt does not involve a moral issue in relation to the purposes for which it is created, the methods by which it is repaid or the rights and legitimate expectations of individuals whom it may affect.

Such a view is untenable in a free society. It rests on the mistaken idea that there can exist side by side in it two principles governing the making and keeping of promises. The one is applicable to the private sector in which individuals are supposed to be legally and morally obliged to repay debt. The other is supposed to apply in the public sector where Government can discharge or fail to discharge its obligation, to repay its debts, as it sees fit.

But the keeping of promises and the honouring of obligations, voluntarily assumed, involves only one principle. Morality in the free monetary order is indivisible.

In this book I have rejected the nominalist conception of public monetary obligations according to which they can be abrogated at the dictates of convenience and expediency. I have argued that it leads to the destruction of trust in the monetary order. It is significant that, whereas the nineteenth century was greatly concerned to fashion safeguards against the over-optimistic extension of private credit and its subsequent excessive contraction, today it is generally assumed that Governments can be left to be the sole arbiters in regard to the extent to which they create both debt and the money to "repay" it. Only in the U.S.A. and a few other countries are there still constitutional provisions to protect the monetary order from the whims of legislatures or from the authorities which have supplanted them.

I wish, once again, to stress that the basic issue is not one of relative efficiency or inefficiency of Government or its agents in conducting particular enterprises or providing particular services. It is whether the principle of accountability should hold for Governments or whether they should be permitted to escape the sanction of economic failure by depreciating the currency.

That sanction, for all engaged in business or private economic transactions, is the need to honour monetary obligations through the successful conduct of affairs. The sanction following upon failure is automatic. In the case of Government there is no such sanction.

There are those who believe that the distrust of the monetary order which results from the depreciation of the currency as a result of irresponsible government policies, or those forced upon it by sectional interests, need cause little concern. They argue that the consequent distrust of money can be overcome by technical expedients. These comprise such well known devices as indexed loans, escalator clauses, future contracts and the re-casting of business accounts to reflect assumed future rates of inflation or to correct past ones. But however necessary such devices may be in times of monetary turmoil, those who think *distrust* can be overcome thereby are labouring under an illusion. If you distrust a person you cannot get to trust him by devising traps and stratagems against a breach of trust by him. Your distrust will continue because of your fear that he may defeat them with new ones of his own.

This, of course, is actually what businesses and individuals have so often experienced when they have sought methods of protecting their income and assets from inflation: Governments have simply responded by passing new and often retrospective legislation to nullify them. What the advocates of such expedients overlook is that trust or mistrust relate to the character not only of persons but also of institutions.

The Civil Condition

The fact is that many modern Governments are much weaker than is assumed. We have seen how dependent monetary order is on the heritage, the outlook, the ideology and the customs of the community. In the last half-century national governments have, owing to changes in these, been under increasing pressure in regard to monetary policies which they have been too weak to control or to resist. The ambivalence towards a free monetary order is, as I have shown, the result of very complex factors. It is basically due to a deep division of opinion as to its meaning and significance. There are those who support the principles which are essential if individuals are to escape from paternalism and restrictive authority. They wish to have the full responsibility of individual choice and to honour the obligations it involves. They regard individual trial and error in the face of uncertainty as something which society cannot escape but only, at its peril, limit, cabin and confine.

There are others – and their numbers have been increasing in many countries – who reject this view. They contend that, because everything is uncertain, individuals cannot really *know* whether a particular economic enterprise should or should not be undertaken. They argue, therefore, that the Government's guess is as good as anyone else's: all should be equally absolved from responsibility for failure, since only fate and circumstance determine the outcome. To hold individuals accountable is consequently irrelevant and so also, they believe, is the free-exchange economy. On this view, personal moral responsibility in decision-making is of no consequence. Economic choices are just occurrences – like the birth of the baby which the parents announced by saying: "A baby arrived", as if no one at all had been responsible for the event.

I have already examined the error involved in this simplistic interpretation. It arises from thinking of knowledge as existing ready at hand, whereas it has to be sought by different individuals and the results of the search subjected to the objective test of the process of exchange.

Even now, most of the people of the world remain untouched by any but the simplest monetary arrangements. They constitute the Third World of money and have always done so.[15] Their lives are regulated within a narrower circle of loyalties than those in the advanced money economies whose operations span the globe. There have also, it is worth remembering, been societies which once dominated the world economy of their time by means of their trustworthy monetary arrangements but failed to maintain them and eventually found that the monetary traffic of the world had passed them by.

What I am concerned to emphasize is that any free monetary order is a way of civic life. Like all free political associations it involves burdens which individuals or societies may be unwilling, unprepared or unable to assume: rather they may opt for what they believe to be security – even at the expense of freedom. They may desire arrangements where the outcomes of social action seem simpler or more closely related to persons, associations or institutions that appear to guarantee their own or society's safety.

For them, the money economy may seem so abstract that they fear it. Such individuals or societies are likely to approve arrangements which limit the purposes for which money may be used, whether for saving or spending, for investing or hoarding, for oneself or for others, for the young or the old, for sickness or for health, until money becomes, as it has become over vast areas of the world, merely a cloakroom ticket – only valid for the cloakrooms of the State. It is, however, not astonishing that those who from fear reject or abandon a free monetary order, because it rests on the somewhat abstract expression of individual rationality, are most likely to fall victims of nemesis in the form of other abstractions, in particular those of authority and tyranny.

Perhaps this final negation of the free monetary order may serve best to illustrate what it really is: a condition of civility,[16] a code of civil monetary behaviour, an ideal – the pursuit of trust.

APPENDIX 57255

Georg Simmel (1858–1918):
A Biographical Note

Georg Simmel was born in Berlin. He became a lecturer at Berlin in 1885 but, although he was a brilliant teacher much loved and admired by his students and his lectures attracted very large audiences, his academic promotion was slow. The University of Berlin only gave him the title of Extraordinary Professor (Ausserordentlicher Professor), which was an honourable distinction but not a definite position with adequate remuneration. He remained in Berlin until he was called to Strassburg to take up the post of Professor of Philosophy (Ordinarius) in 1914. He accepted it only on financial grounds. That academic promotion and security were so long withheld, was mainly due to Simmel's Jewish ancestry and because he did not identify with any political and social groups. In his view, none granted the individual independence. He could not go along fully with the centralist policies of the Empire or with the abstract *laissez-faire* programme of liberalism which he thought led to the dominance of big business. Although not antagonistic to the worker, he also found himself unable to embrace socialism. He feared its glorification of the masses.

The groups nearest to him, for a short time, were the independent liberal thinkers outside the university. This is shown by two of his earliest publications: *Über Sociale Differenzierung* (1890) and *Einleitung in die Moralwissenschaft* (1892–3). In the earlier of these works, Simmel sees the essence of modern development in the distortion of the substance of society into a sum of inter-relationships of participating individuals. In the later work, which he subsequently rejected, he sought to construct a system of morals describing man's moral life psychologically, without evaluating it. His *Die Probleme des Geschichtsphilosophie* (also 1892), greatly altered by Simmel in later editions, had considerable influence.

Therein he postulated that events must be distinguished from history. The philosophy of history seeks out those *a priori* assumptions of historical consciousness on the foundations on which "the historical world is built". The same idea was pursued in: *Das Problem der historischen Zeit* ("The Problem of Historical Time") and *Vom Wesen des historischen Verstehens* ("The Essence of Historical Comprehension"), which are included in the collection *Brücke und Tür* (1957). He suggests there is no road to objective reality itself, only diverse subjective worlds dependent on their categorical assumptions. Simmel's relativism reached its peak in *Die Philosophie des Geldes* (1900), in which he tried to discover the relation of money to all spheres of our life – its influences on all branches of culture – and expose the spiritual, moral and religious assumptions of historical materialism, in order to overcome it.

Simmel analysed the expression of intellectuality not only in his book *Kant* (1904) but also in *Schopenhauer and Nietzsche* (1907), *Goethe* (1913), *Rembrandt* (1916) and in *Lebensanschauung (Vier metaphysische Kapitel)*. The last was published after his death. His studies on art, religion and philosophy tried to show that each is a world in itself, not a derivative of another, because it depends on special subjective functions of life. In his books *Soziologie* (1908) and *Grundfragen der Soziologie* (1917), as well as in numerous essays, Simmel analyses all processes of association and dissociation as psychic phenomena, but he also constitutes the science of sociology by separating the forms of sociation from their content in such a way that purely formal concepts of relationships become generalizable and thereby scientific in character. They remain constant in a multitude of concrete events.

By all accounts it was on the lecture platform that he most fully realized his manifold talents. Spykman has vividly described his performance on it:

His lectures were not only learned, they were an inspiration. He combined a clear, logical analysis with an artistic, impressionistic approach. A beautiful voice, an excellent diction, an appealing personality, all contributed to the charm of his address. A vivid gesticulation would bring suggestions of life and growth and give real expression to the dynamic quality of his thought. It would vitalize his discourse just where a mere conceptual abstraction seemed cold and rigid and even the best available word weak and inadequate. Form and subject-matter of his lectures were so perfectly adapted that the logical sequences seemed inevitable stages in a natural unfoldment.

He gave his audience more than knowledge. He gave himself, and in so doing he gave of the best of his time. He helped his hearers to live, to find an adaptation to that vast cultural environment which is the European social heritage. Simmel was not only the philosopher of European culture, he was a bearer of that culture, a lover of the best it had to offer. Not only did he know it, he lived it.[1]

The indirect cause of his death, only four years after coming to Strassburg, was the mental shock which his sensitive nature received through the hatred released by the 1914–18 war. He realized that the war threatened the very foundation of European culture. Frenzied patriotism had divided the European philosophers and scientists into national factions concerned not with the pursuit of truth but with political propaganda.

Simmel created no philosophical or sociological school in the narrow sense of the word. He submitted only rarely to the discipline required for systematic exposition of a body of knowledge. This was not due to laziness or arbitrariness. Rather, his method of writing – so often somewhat disjointed – reflected the skill of the teacher intent on shocking his hearers through unusual illustrations and disclosure of unexpected relationships. But there were deeper reasons for his failure to create a school of accepted views. For, as Donald N. Levine has reminded us, Simmel believed that the ultimate justification for scholarship lies in the materials it provides for the cultivation of educated individuals.

Both philosophical and personal temperament caused Simmel not only to describe but also to pursue the ideal of authentic individuality. In his diary at the end of his life he wrote: "I know that I shall die without intellectual heirs, and that is as it should be. My legacy will be like cash, distributed to many heirs, each transforming his part into use according to *his* nature – a use which will no longer reveal its indebtedness to this heritage."[2]

For sources of this Note see:

Nicholas J. Spykman, *The Social Theory of Georg Simmel*, 1925, New York. Reissued, 1964. (Includes list of similar writings and books.)

Kurt H. Wolff, Introduction to *The Sociology of Georg Simmel*, 1950, Glencoe, Illinois.

Paul Honigsheim, "The Time and Thought of the Young Simmel," in *Georg Simmel, 1858–1918* (ed.), Kurt H. Wolff, p. 167.

Donald N. Levine, Introduction to *Georg Simmel on Individuality and Social Forms*, 1971, Chicago and London.
Samuel Hugo Bergman and Werner J. Cahnman. Article on "Georg Simmel" in *Encyclopaedia Judaica*, vol. 14, p. 1575.

Books on Georg Simmel

H. Liebeschütz, *Von G. Simmel zu F. Rosenzweig* (1970).
L. Coser, *Georg Simmel* (1965), which includes a list of his works.
R. H. Weingartner, *Experience and Culture: the Philosophy of Georg Simmel*, (1962), which includes a bibliography; K. H. Wolff (ed.), *Georg Simmel, 1858–1918*. A collection of essays with translations and a bibliography (1959).
M. Susman, *Die geistige Gestalt G. Simmels* (1959).
K. Gassen and M. Landmann (ed.), *Buch des Dankes an Georg Simmel* (1959).

Notes

NOTES TO INTRODUCTION

1. Edmund Burke: *Works*, Rivington edition, vol. V, 1826–7, p. 122. Quoted by Charles Parkin, *The Moral Basis of Burke's Political Thought*, Cambridge University Press, 1956.
2. S. Herbert Frankel: *The Economic Impact on Under-Developed Societies: Essays on International Investment and Social Change*, Basil Blackwell, Oxford and Harvard University Press, Mass. 1953.
3. S. Herbert Frankel, op. cit., p. 31.
4. Sir Isaiah Berlin: "Does Political Theory still Exist?" in *Philosophy, Politics and Society* (Second Series), Peter Laslett and W. G. Runciman (eds.), Basil Blackwell, Oxford 1969, p. 4 ff.
5. Henry Simons: "Rules versus Authorities in Monetary Policy", in *Journal of Political Economy*, vol. 44 (1936). Reprinted in *Readings in Monetary Theory*, American Economic Association, vol. V, p. 363.
6. Henry Simons, op. cit., p. 356.
7. Milton Friedman: "The Role of Monetary Policy", Presidential Address to the American Economic Association, 29 December 1967; *American Economic Review*, March 1968 (reprinted in *The Optimum Quantity of Money and other Essays*, Aldine Publishing, 1969, pp. 95–110; quotation p. 99).
8. A. I. Melden: *Rights and Right Conduct*, Oxford 1959, p. 13.
9. Georg Simmel: *Die Philosophie des Geldes*. Second Edition, Duncker and Humblot, Leipzig 1907.
10. Cf. K. Peter Etzkorn: "Georg Simmel: An Introduction", p. 2, in *Georg Simmel: The Conflict in Modern Culture and Other Essays* translated by K. Peter Etzkorn, Teachers College Press, New York. This sentence occurs in the context of the following passage:

For Simmel, the continuity of the processes of life, clashes necessarily with the acts of personal individuation, which are also the creative acts in which social institutions are established. These, in turn, gain a reality of their own which transcends their immediate *raison d'être*. Frequently in this process, what originally were considered as means come to be regarded as ends. . . . This process, however, always occurs for Simmel within the framework of social relations regardless of specific historical periods. The dialectic is neither characteristic of capitalism, nor of socialism, nor of liberal democracy; it is much more. For Simmel, this dialectic between life and more-than-life represents the very nature of human existence, the very destiny of civilization, and thus it becomes the core of his scholarly inquiry".

11. Cf. Karl Popper: *The Poverty of Historicism*, Routledge & Kegan Paul, Second Edition, London 1960, pp. 69–70. He also pointed out that:"It seems to escape the well-meaning Utopianist that this programme implies an admission of failure, even before he launches it. For it substitutes for his demand that we build a new society, fit for men and women to live in, the demand that we 'mould' these men and women to fit into his new society."

NOTES TO CHAPTER I

1. Wesley C. Mitchell: *The Backward Art of Spending Money and other Essays*, New York 1950, p. 170. Reprinted from *American Economic Review* vol. VI, Supplement, March 1916. I am indebted to Professor W. Breit for drawing my attention to the significance of this article.
2. S. P. Altmann: *American Journal of Sociology,* 1903. Altmann was one of the first reviewers of Georg Simmel's book, *Die Philosophie des Geldes.*
3. G. M. Trevelyan in his *English Social History*, London 1942, writes: "The interval between the Great Reform Bill of 1832 and the end of the nineteenth century may, if we like, be called the Victorian Age". But he added "We must not think of these seventy years as having a fixed likeness one to another, merely because more than sixty of them were presided over by 'the Queen' (1837-1901). If any unity is to be ascribed to the Victorian era in England, it must be found in two governing conditions: first, there was no great war and no fear of catastrophe from without: and secondly the whole period was marked by interest in religious questions and was deeply influenced by seriousness of thought and self-discipline of character, an outcome of the Puritan ethos" (p. 509).

4. Mitchell, op. cit., p. 168. Mitchell went on to point out that: "In thus singling out the use of money as bringing system into economic behavior, as providing the basis for exact analysis, current theory is returning to the starting point from which Cournot set out on his researches in 1838. What we call price, what Cournot calls the 'abstract idea of *wealth* or of *value of exchange*,' he explains, in his first chapter, is 'suited for the foundation of a scientific theory,' because it is 'a definite idea, and consequently susceptible of rigorous treatment in combinations.' This abstract idea of wealth 'could not have been grasped by men of Teutonic stock, either at the epoch of the Conquest, or even at much later periods, when the feudal law existed in full vigor. . . . Such an idea of wealth as we draw from our advanced state of civilization, and such as is necessary to give rise to a theory, can only be slowly developed as a consequence of the progress of commercial relations.' A remarkable anticipation of the outcome of two generations of hard thinking! And Cournot applies his insight: as a first problem he chooses not barter, but foreign exchange – the kind of transaction in which nothing but pecuniary factors are involved." (The reference is to A. Cournot: *Researches into the Mathematical Principles of the Theory of Wealth*, 1838, translation by N. T. Bacon, New York and London 1897, Chaps. I and III.)

5. Ibid, p. 173.

6. Rudolph H. Weingartner, in his essay "Form and Content in Simmel's 'Philosophy of Life' " (in *Georg Simmel, 1858–1918: A Collection of Essays*, edited by Kurt H. Wolff, op. cit., elucidates what Simmel means by this as follows:

Life as more-life expresses the fact that life is a self-perpetuating process. ". . . As long as life exists at all, it produces something living," namely, more of itself. But life's productivity does not end with its creation of more life. It creates and sets free from itself something that is not life but "which has its own significance and follows its own law." Because of this attribute of life, Simmel adds a second defining expression: "life is more-than-life." This "more-than-life" refers to the objects which life creates by virtue of the formal principles implicit in experience. Whether we consider contents only as they are shaped *in* experience, whether we focus upon an ideal world that is implicitly *generated* by experience or whether we attend to a human work as a material *embodiment* of experience, the structure in question "possesses its own meaning, a logical coherence, some kind of validity or stability independent of its having been produced which are the conditions of the creation of objects by life, guarantee, at the same time, the emancipation of the created from the creator." (Simmel: *Lebes-anschauungen,* p. 20.)

7. Nicholas J. Spykman: *The Social Theory of Georg Simmel,* Russell & Russell Inc., New York 1964, pp. 249–51.

8. Ibid., p. 251.

9. Simmel wrote in the same Preface:

Not one line of these investigations is meant to be a statement about economics. That is to say, the phenomena of valuation and purchase, of exchange and the means of exchange, of the forms of production and the values of possession, which economics views from one standpoint, are here viewed from another. . . . One science . . . never exhausts the total of a reality. . . . Exchange can . . . legitimately be handled as a psychological, as a moral-historical, and even as an aesthetic fact. . . . Here [in this book] money is only a means, material, or example, for the depicting of relations that link the most superficial, "realistic", and accidental phenomena . . . with the deepest currents of the life of the individual and of history.

10. G. Schmoller: *Simmel's Philosophie des Geldes*; Schmoller's *Jahrbücher* 1901–3.

11. Duncan adds:

Our present concern with interaction is but one example of this. When we talk about interaction, what exactly are we talking about? How do we study it? *What are the data of interaction?* Over a half-century has passed since Simmel began his description of interaction; yet we still go on talking about social structure with little reference to function. Common sense teaches us that we "function" in role enactment through *symbolic* interaction whose societal meanings arise *in* communication. We do not "have" meanings and then share them. On the contrary, as we communicate we create meanings. What we know about motivation is derived from what is said about it. We can argue that symbols are but a terministic screen . . . which lies beyond our reality in terms of physical or human nature. But wherever we assign our causes, when we return to specifically *human* experience we must deal with *expressions* of these causes in *symbols.* In his discussion of knowledge, truth, and falsehood in human relations, Simmel says: "Human interaction is normally based on the fact that the ideational worlds of men have certain elements in common, that objective intellectual contents constitute the material which is transformed into subjective life by means of men's social relations. . . ." Thus while he argued that the science of sociology must concern itself with structure, he did *not* mean mechanical or biological but *symbolic* structure as we know it in art and play.

Cf. "Simmel's Image of Society", in Kurt H. Wolff (Editor): Georg Simmel 1858–1918, Ohio State University Press, 1959, pp. 108–9.

12. Cf. The Preface to Georg Simmel, *Die Philosophie des Geldes*, op. cit.

13. Spykman observes that Simmel analyses society:

In terms of component elements, not as individual existences, but as bearers of relationships. It is an analysis in terms of functions, not in terms of substances; it is an analysis in terms of relationships, not in terms of individuals. Society as content is the totality, is the sum of all individuals, together with all their interests and all their relationships and all the products which result from the transformations of these interests through their realization in socialization. But society as form, as association, is nothing but the sum of the integrating functional relationships.

(op. cit. p. 88). Spykman elsewhere also writes that Simmel's thought:

is very similar to that underlying modern mathematics. To see a form or a category in its relation to life is not to dissolve it, but to see it as a function relative to a system of reference. A function of one or more variables is not something inferior to a constant because, as quantity, it is variable. That would be to misunderstand its essence, which is not quantity, but relationship.

The essential characteristic of a function is not variability of quantity, but constancy of relationship.

(op. cit. p. 21).

14. Gilbert Ryle: *The Concept of Mind*, Hutchinson University Library, London 1949 p. 16.

15. Cf. E. V. Walter, *Simmel's Sociology of Power: The Architecture of Politics* (p. 159) in Kurt H. Wolff (ed.) *Georg Simmel 1858–1918*, loc. cit. Walter also quotes the following passage from Simmel:

It is a fact of the greatest sociological importance that innumerable relationships preserve their sociological structure unchanged, even after the feeling or practical occasion, which originally gave rise to them, has ended. Sociological connectedness, no matter what its origin, develops a self-preservation and autonomous existence of its form that are independent of its initially connecting motives. Without this inertia of existing sociations, society as a whole would constantly collapse, or change in an unimaginable fashion.

16. Simmel: *Philosophie des Geldes*, op. cit., pp. 86–7.

17. Cf. Matthew Lipman: "Some Aspects of Simmel's Conception of the Individual" in *Georg Simmel 1858–1918*, Karl H. Wolff (ed.), op. cit., p. 128.

Ibid. He added (p. 129):

What the eighteenth century failed to understand was that the emancipation of men from an oppressive social system, in the name of equality,
would lead directly to the oppression of men by one another, also in the
name of equality. Unless the freedom of the strong is restricted (through
law or the ethics of fraternalism), the strong restrict the freedom of the
weak. An equal measure of freedom for all, therefore, leads to inequality,
to the concentration of power and the monopolization of opportunities.

The eighteenth century may have had some fleeting faith that the spirit of
fraternity would resolve this antinomy between equality and freedom. But
it pinned its hopes on the notion of law. The individual is to be conceived of
as an instance of a general rule. That which differentiates the particular case
is merely accidental, external, trivial. The essence of man, his humanity,
lives in each individual, is an atomic unit, everywhere alike, and absolutely
amenable to universal law. Because this unconditionally identical core in all
men finds its freedom in submitting to the requirements of universatility, in
lawful rather than lawless behavior, men themselves achieve freedom by
liberating the humanity within them. To be moral is to deny yourself
privileges which you might ordinarily take on the grounds that you are
different from others. In this view, articulated most clearly in Kant, to be
moral is to submit oneself to universal law, and to be lawful is to be free.

18. The quotation from Simmel is from his essay on "Individual
and Society in Eighteenth- and Nineteenth-Century Views of Life"
in the translation by Kurt H. Wolff (ed.): *The Sociology of Georg
Simmel*, The Free Press, Glencoe, Illinois, 1950, p. 83.

19. Fernand Braudel: *Capitalism and Material Life 1400–1800*,
Weidenfeld and Nicolson, London 1973.

20. Simmel; *Philosophie des Geldes,* op. cit., pp. 164–5.

NOTES TO CHAPTER II

1. *The Sociology of Georg Simmel*, edited by Kurt H. Wolff, op.
cit., p. 409.

2. For a full account see S. E. Harris: *The Assignats*, Harvard
University Press, 1930, p. 8.

3. Ibid., p. 8. Harris wrote:

It was thought that this paper money could be made acceptable in the eyes
of the unsophisticated public by being attached to special advantages in the
purchase of lands. Actually, of course, it was issued as a matter of pure
expediency. To make it acceptable to the unsuspecting man in the street he

was subjected to "a thorough system of propaganda and education" which made him believe "that the Revolutionary paper money was not a replica of Law's paper money of unhappy memory".

4. Charles Rist quotes (p. 103 ff.) from Cantillon, Hume, Turgot, Adam Smith, Thornton and Ricardo to support his contention that this disparagement of the role of money was chiefly a reaction against John Law, who had made money the source of all wealth. I have made use of the excellent account and analysis in his classic *History of Monetary and Credit Theory from John Law to the Present Day*. Translated from the French edition of 1938 by Jane Degras, George Allen & Unwin, London 1940. This remarkable work is, in my opinion, as relevant today as when it was first written.

5. Quoted by Rist (p. 64) from *John Law's Troisième Lettre sur le Nouvea Système des Finances*, "as a warning to all who believe it possible, in matters of exchange, *to substitute compulsion for agreement freely arrived at*" (italics added). It is indeed ironical to note today a comparison Rist drew between his time and age (nearly 50 years ago!) and the eighteenth century. "No other epoch", he wrote, "has given more forcible expression to its disdain for metallic money, a mere medium of exchange and contemptible like all middlemen. The contradiction . . . between the philosophers' disregard for gold, and the passionate search, on the part both of governments and individuals, for means of acquiring as much of it as possible, is just as striking in the eighteenth century as it is in our own day" (p. 103).

6. *Principles of Political Economy*, edited by W. J. Ashley, 1928, p. 488 (italics added).

7. For an account of the literature of dissent from this view see Arthur Wolfgang Cohn: *Kann das Geld abgeschafft werden?*, Verlag von Gustav Fischer, Jena 1920.

8. Keynes: John Maynard Keynes: *The General Theory of Employment Interest and Money in Collected Writings*, The Royal Economic Society, London, vol. VII, p. 366.

9. Karl Marx: *Early Writings*, ed. T. B. Bottomore, London 1963, p. 37.

10. Cf. *1844 Early Manuscripts*, p. 119.

11. This sentence is quoted by Graeme Duncan from *Marx's Grundrisse*, selected and translated by D. McLellan, London 1971, p. 161.

12. Summarized from John Plamenatz: *Karl Marx's Philosophy of Man*, Clarendon Press, Oxford 1975, p. 122.

13. Paul Craig Roberts and Mathew A. Stephenson: *Marx's Theory of Exchange, Alienation and Crisis*, Hoover Institution Press, Stanford University, California 1973, p. 2.

14. On this Roberts and Stephenson comment:

When Marx finds that man is alienated under commodity production, he is comparing him both to a past state and to a future one. In neither pre- nor post-capitalist systems is there a separation between production and use. Instead there is directly associated production with convivial relations between men and community control over economic life. Some have interpreted Marx's scheme in terms of fall and redemption. It is partially redemptive in that the convivial relations and community control over production which were destroyed by exchange are supposed to be restored under communism, but the basis for the directly associated production is different in pre- and post-capitalist systems. In a pre-capitalist system conviviality is rooted in community tradition and ritual; in the post-capitalist system it is rooted in a scientific consciousness. Since economic life controls human consciousness, society cannot have control over itself until it controls its economic life. Under capitalism, the control man gains over nature through technology is offset by the control his economic organization has over him (op. cit., p. 76).

15. Roberts and Stephenson, op. cit., p. 13.

16. Quoted by Roberts and Stephenson (op. cit., p. 16) from Karl Marx: *Pre-Capitalist Economic Formations*, International Publishers, New York 1965, p. 96.

17. Karl Marx: *Capital*, p. 77. The full passage is quoted by Roberts and Stephenson, op. cit., p. 45.   18. Ibid.

19. Graeme Duncan: *Marx and Mill: Two Views of Social Conflict and Social Harmony*, Cambridge University Press, 1973, p. 82.

20. Graeme Duncan, ibid., p. 112 (quoted from *Capitalism*, p. 592).

21. R. H. Weingartner: *Experience and Culture*, Wesleyan University Press, 1962, p. 84.

22. The term is Weingartner's, op. cit., p. 72. He writes: "Simmel's term is 'culture' (Kultur), Although . . . he uses it to refer to the process which is usually indicated by the term *Bildung*."

23. Weingartner, op. cit., p. 72.

24. Charles Taylor: *Hegel*, Cambridge University Press, 1975, p. 382. Taylor continues: "These institutions and practices make up the public life of a society. Certain norms are implicit in them, which they demand to be maintained and properly lived out. Because of

what voting is as a concatenating procedure of social decision, certain norms about falsification, the autonomy of the individual decision, etc. flow inescapably from it. The norms of a society's public life are the content of *Sittlichkeit*. This term Taylor translates in the Glossary to the book (p. xi) as "ethical – as a Hegelian term of art designating the morality which holds of us in virtue of being members of a self-subsistent community, to which we owe allegiance as an embodiment of the universal".

25. Spykman, op. cit., p. 246.

26. Cf. Paul Honigsheim: "A Note on Simmel's Anthropological Interests", in *Georg Simmel 1858–1918*, op. cit., see p. 177, and *Philosophie des Geldes* (see p. 383 ff.).

27. Summarized from Spykman, op. cit., p. 131.

28. Simmel observed that voting

is a projection of real forces and of their proportions upon the plane of *intellectuality*; it anticipates, in an abstract symbol, the result of concrete battle and coercion". Moreover in his view voting illustrates also the *tragic nature* of social existence, for the minority must not only yield but must positively participate in the action which was decided on against its will and conviction. The unifrom character of the decision contains no trace of the minority's dissent and even makes it responsible for the decision, which thus becomes "the most poignant expression of the dualism between the autonomous life of the individual and the life of society, a dualism which is often harmonized in experience, but which, in principle, is irreconcilable"

(cf. E. V. Walter, "Simmel's Sociology of Power: The Architecture of Politics", in Kurt H. Wolff (ed.), *Georg Simmel 1858–1918*, op. cit., p. 145 (italics added)).

29. Cf. Spykman's "Summary and Interpretation of Simmel's Views", op. cit., pp. 234–6, and see *Philosophie des Geldes*, pp. 480–501.

30. This has been pointed out in Zvi Woislawski's valuable study *Simmels Philosophie des Kapitalistischen Geistes* (Thesis submitted to the Faculty of Philosophy, University of Berlin, February 1931) to which I am greatly indebted for many insights into and references to Simmel's meaning and works. It has been translated into Hebrew and published under the transliterated title *Mishnat Zimmel 'al ruah ha-rekhushanut*, Jerusalem 1966 (Library of Congress HG221. S6W6).

31. The quotation from Simmel is from Kurt H. Wolff (ed.), *The Sociology of Georg Simmel*, op. cit., p. 309.

32. The phrase is Simmel's. I am indebted to Matthew Lipman: ("Some Aspects of Simmel's Conception of the Individual", in *Georg Simmel 1858–1918*, Karl H. Wolff, ed., Ohio State University Press, 1959) for the analysis of eighteenth- and nineteenth-century attitudes.

33. I am indebted to Professor Peter Heath for suggestions in regard thereto.

34. Moses Hess: "Über das Geldwesen" in *Rheinische Jahrbücher zur Gesellschaftlichen Reform*, vol. I, p. 2. The reader is referred for details in regard to its composition to Edmund Silberner: *Moses Hess. Geschichte seines Lebens*, E. J. Brill, Leiden 1966, pp. 184–93. I have drawn on Silberner's brilliant book for this account.

35. Sir Isaiah Berlin: *The Life and Opinions of Moses Hess*, W. Heffer & Sons Limited, Cambridge, England 1959, p. 45. He added (p. 46):

Even though he knew that he would be mercilessly denounced for stupidity, ignorance and irresponsible utopianism by his admired, tyrannical comrades in arms, Marx and Engels, Hess could not bring himself to view the world through their distorting spectacles. He did not accept their view of man's nature. He believed in the permanent and universal validity of certain general human values. To the end of his days he firmly believed that human feeling, natural affections, the desire for social justice, individual freedom and solidarity within historically continuous groups – families or religious associations or nationalities – were to be valued as being good in themselves. He did not think that these deep human interests, however they might be modified in space or time, were necessarily altered by historical evolution or conditioned by class consciousness or by any other relatively transient phenomenon to anything like the decisive extent of which the so-called scientific Marxists spoke.

36. Silberner, op. cit., p. 659 ff.

NOTES TO CHAPTER III

1. Walter Bagehot: *Lombard Street: A Description of the Money Market*, London 1873, p. 68.

2. "Of the greatness of the power there will be no doubt. Money is economical power. Everyone is aware that England is the greatest moneyed country in the world; everyone admits that it has much more immediately disposable and ready cash than any other coun-

try. But very few persons are aware *how much* greater the ready balance – the floating loan-fund which can be lent to anyone or for any purpose – is in England than it is anywhere else in the world." He goes on to show that the deposits of banks which published their accounts were about twice as large in London in 1872 than those in Paris, New York and the German Empire taken together. The deposits of banks in Britain which did not publish their accounts were far greater still (p. 4, ibid., italics added).

3.

Of course the deposits of bankers are not a strictly accurate measure of the resources of a Money Market. On the contrary, much more cash exists out of banks in France and Germany, and in all non-banking countries, than could be found in England or Scotland, where banking is developed. But that cash is not, so to speak, "Money-Market money": *it is not attainable.* Nothing but their immense misfortunes, nothing but a vast loan in their own securities, could have extracted the hoards of France from the custody of the French people. The offer of no other securities would have tempted them, for they had confidence in no other securities. For all other purposes the money hoarded was useless and might as well not have been hoarded. But the English money is "borrowable" money.

(pp. 5–6, ibid., italics added.)

4. Ibid., p. 68 (italics added).

5. Cf. Carl Menger: *Problems of Economics and Sociology*, ed., Louis Schneider, trans., Francis J. Nock, University of Illinois Press, Urbana 1963, p. 155. This is a translation of *Untersuchungen über die Methode der Socialwissenschaften und der Politischen Oekonomie Insbesondere*, Leipzig 1883.

Pure barter, he suggested, contained within itself a very effective means of escape from its limiting constraints. This he described as follows:

Each individual could easily observe that there was a greater demand in the market for certain wares, namely those which fitted a very general need, than there was for others. . . . These others were ones which he, to be sure, did not need at the moment, but which were more marketable than his. By this he did not, of course, directly attain the final goal of his planned economic operation (procuring by exchange the goods *he* needed!), but he approached it essentially. The economic interest of the economic individuals, therefore, with increased knowledge of their *individual* interests, without any agreement, without legislative compulsion, *even without any consideration of public interest*, leads them to turn over their wares for more marketable ones, even if they do not need the latter for their immediate consumer needs. Among the latter, however, as is readily evident, they again select those which are most easily and most economically suited to the function of a means of barter. Thus there appears before us, under the powerful influence of custom the phenomenon to be observed everywhere with advancing economic culture that a certain number of goods are accepted in exchange by everybody. . . . They are goods which our predecessors called *Geld,* from *gelten,* i.e. to perform, to "pay".

(ibid., p. 154).

6. James Bonar: *Philosophy & Political Economy in Some of their Historical Relations*, London 1893.

7. Menger: op. cit., p. 155.

8. Ibid., pp. 227–8. He added:

When the population becomes aware of the idea of community, when it gradually begins to feel that it is one, then the sphere of its interests expands and with it that of its rules of law. They cease to be the mere result of the efforts of the people of the nation directed toward protection of the *individual interest.* Also the *common interest*, or what is considered that, enters the mental sphere of the population and with it the awareness of the necessity for protecting this interest against individual despotism. To law which results from the effort of individuals to assure their individual achievements is added law which is the result of efforts directed toward the protection of the community. But this is not necessarily the fruit of common counsel, either, of an agreement, of a contract, or of positive legislation. Its origin is analogous to that of national law in general.

9. Menger's view is analogous to that of Edmund Burke, who wrote "in all our changes, there are enough of the old to preserve unbroken the traditionary chain of the maxims and policy of our ancestors . . . and enough of the new to invigorate us and bring us to our true character by being taken fresh from the mass of the people" (*Works*, loc. cit., vol. 3, p. 75; quoted by Parkin: op. cit., p. 51.

10. Menger: op. cit., pp. 229–30. The above quotation is from a paragraph which begins as follows:

However, law can also come into being, . . . by *authority*. The man in power or intellectually superior can set certain limits to the discretion of the weak. . . . The victor can set certain limits for the vanquished. He can impose on them certain rules for their action to which they have to submit, without considering their free conviction: from fear. These rules . . . are both by origin and by the guarantees of their realization essentially different from the law which grows out of the convictions of the population. . . . Indeed, they can be in direct contrast to national law; they are really *statute*, not *law*. But the strong man has an interest in calling them "law", in cloaking them with the sanctity of law, in connecting them with religious traditions, in elevating them so that they become the objects of religious and ethical education. This is the case until the habit of obedience and the sense of subjection developed by them recognize in them something analogous to law and until this habit and sense scarcely distinguish any longer those rules limiting the discretion of the individual which are produced by the convictions of the nation from those which power prescribes for the weak [italics added].

11. See ch. V, p. 63 below for the quotation from R. F. Harrod concerning Keynes from which these words are taken.

12. F. A. Hayek: "Law, Legislation and Liberty", in *Rules and Order*, Routledge & Kegan Paul, London, vol. 1, 1973, pp. 10–11. Hayek added:

This intentionalist or pragmatic account of history found its fullest expression in the conception of the formation of society by a social contract, first in Hobbes and then in Rousseau, who in many respects was a direct follower of Descartes. Even though their theory was not always meant as a historical account of what actually happened, it was always meant to provide a guideline for deciding whether or not existing institutions were to be approved as rational. It is to this philosophical conception that we owe the preference which prevails to the present day for everything that is done "consciously" or "deliberately", and from it the terms "irrational" or "non-rational" derive the derogatory meaning they now have. Because of this the earlier presumption in favour of traditional or established institutions and usages became a presumption against them, and "opinion" came to be thought of as "mere" opinion – something not demonstrable or decidable by reason and therefore not to be accepted as a valid ground for decision.

13. Menger went on to point out that the repeated debasements of the currency by the masters of the mints soon caused the ordinary weights of bullion and the weights according to which the precious metals were used in trade (i.e. counted out in the form of coins) to become very different. This fact contributed not a little toward causing money to be wrongly regarded "as a special measure of exchange value even though the standard coin in every natural economy is nothing but a unit of weight defined by the weight according to which the precious metals are traded". Menger: op. cit., pp. 282–3.

14. *Problems of Economics and Sociology*, p. 227.

15. "In so far as an ideology attempts to marshal a group to attain a particular aim, its adoption necessarily represents a commitment by

the group sharing it. The word (aim) may be quite rigidly confined, to mean more a projection than a reality; but, if it is so confined, it should not be overlooked that the preservation of a reality may equally be projected, and thus become the object of an ideology. The point of all this, however, is that an ideology does not possess an exclusively logical or philosophical character at all". Cf. Preston King: "An Ideological Fallacy", in *Politics and Experience: Essays Presented to Professor Michael Oakeshott on the Occasion of his Retirement*, ed. Preston King and B. C. Parekh, Cambridge University Press, London 1968, p. 353.

16. John Rawls: "Justice as Fairness", in *Philosophical Review*, 1958. Reprinted in *Philosophy, Politics and Society*, Second Series, ed. Peter Laslett and W. G. Runciman, Blackwell, Oxford 1969, p. 139.

17. Schumpeter in his *History of Economic Analysis* (op. cit., p. 1115) recognized the importance of Macleod's contribution in the following passages: ". . . the first – though not wholly successful – attempt at working out a systematic theory that fits the facts of bank credit adequately, which was made by Macleod, attracted little attention, still less favourable attention". He added: "Henry Dunning Macleod was an economist of many merits who somehow failed to achieve recognition, or even to be taken quite seriously, owing to his inability to put his many good ideas in a professionally acceptable form." He was the author of *The Theory and Practice of Banking*, London 1855, and himself a banker, keenly aware of the nemesis of monetary excesses.

18. He was also ahead of his time in perceiving that what Keynes called "speculative balances" are the most important part of monetary demand. This idea was developed by Carl Menger again much later, and further developed recently by Erich W. Streissler. In his *Theory of Credit*, vol. II, part II, second edition, 1871, p. 892, Macleod wrote, in regard to John Law:

LAWISM is nothing indeed but the fundamental error that Money represents commodities, and that Paper Currency may be based upon commodities. . . . Money does not represent commodities at all, but only Debt, or services due, which have not yet received their equivalent in commodities . . . when the exchanges of Products and Services exactly balance each other there is no need nor use for Money. The use and the necessity for Money only arise when the exchanges of Products and Services are *unequal*: and there remains a Balance or Debt due from Unequal Exchange. The use and the purpose and the necessity for Money is to measure, record and transfer the Debt, or Right to demand some equivalent for services rendered, *at some future time*. A whole line of writers, Philosophical, Literary, Juridical and Economical, have shown that Money is a Bill of Exchange, a Right of Titel to demand at some future time an equivalent for services previously rendered. . . .

19. The words are Schumpeter's in *History of Economic Analysis*, loc. cit., p. 717. They are part of the following passage:

. . . logically, it is by no means clear that the most useful method is to start from the coin – even if, making a concession to realism, we add inconvertible government paper – in order to proceed to the credit transactions of reality. It may be more useful to start from these in the first place, to look upon capitalist finance as a clearing system that cancels claims and debts and carries forward the differences – so that "money" payments come in only as a special case without any particularly fundamental importance. In other words: practically and analytically, a credit theory of money is possibly preferable to a monetary theory of credit.

20. H. D. Macleod: *The Principles of Economical Philosophy*, vol. I, second edition, London 1872, p. 198. It is not justified to accuse Macleod of confusing money and credit. He was often at pains to emphasize the distinction. Any apparent confusion is due to the fact that he wanted to emphasize that all money depends on the confidence with which it can be regarded by the users. Macleod was a pioneer in drawing explicit attention to the phenomenon described by Keynes when he wrote: "acknowledgements of debt are themselves a serviceable substitute for Money – Proper in the settlement of transactions". A substitute, however, must not be confused with money itself.

21. Charles Rist in his *History of Monetary and Credit Theory*, pp. 101–2, wrote: "The idea that the value of the precious metals has a fiduciary character is in fact extremely old. He quotes from A. Wagner's *Beiträge zur Lehre von den Banken*, (Leipzig 1857, p. 38) "that the use of gold rests in part on the confidence of people that it will always serve as a means of purchase". Wagner added: "It is therefore correct to say of every kind of money, and *consequently of metallic money*, that, as distinct from barter, it presupposes a certain development of public confidence, from which it follows that every money rests in part on credit." The same idea was expressed a little later by Macleod. In his evidence before the Committee on Indian Currency in 1899 (see *Official Papers*, A. Marshall, p. 269), Mar-

shall, trying to find those points in monetary theory on which economists are agreed, declared: "I think it is also agreed that there is something fiduciary in the value of gold and silver; that is, that part of their value depends upon the confidence with which people generally look forward to the maintenance and extension of the monetary demand for them." Rist also observes how misleading it is to regard the word fiduciary as somehow derogatory. Thus he wrote: "Others insist on the "fiduciary" character of the value which we give to gold, as if by doing so they were reducing its importance. François Simiand said: 'Gold was the first of the fiduciary moneys.' Though his words were immediately hailed as a discovery, it is an old saying. Marshall, Knut Wicksell, A. Wagner, and many others had already used it. The words seem to imply a denunciation of something artificial or imaginary in the value given to gold by the public, and the 'reasonable' man derives some satisfaction from them. A closer examination, however, will show that *all values have a fiduciary character*, for they are all based on the belief that the *conditions which impart a value to a good will be perpetuated in the future*."

22. *Oeuvres*, vol. V, Maudit Argent, p. 60.

23. Ibid., Macleod, *The Principles of Economical Philosophy*, p. 192.

24. R. S. Peters: *The Concept of Motivation*, London, Routledge & Kegan Paul, 1960, p. 5.

25. *Philosophie des Geldes*, p. 165.

26. On this see the illuminating contribution by Stanley Cavell: "The Avoidance of Love. A Reading of King Lear," in *Must we Mean What we Say? A Book of Essays*, Charles Scribner & Sons, New York 1969.

27. Niklas Luhmann: *Vertrauen ein Mechanismus der Reduktion Socialer Komplexität*, Ferdinand Enke Verlag, Stuttgart, 1968, see especially p. 187.

28. Luhmann, *Vertrauen*, op. cit., p. 23, quoted by Lohmann from Simmel (Georg): *Uber die Formen der Vergesellschaftung*, second edition, Leipzig 1922, p. 263 f.

29. Cf. Luhmann, op. cit., chapter 7.

30. Luhmann, *Vertrauen*, op. cit., p. 67.

31. Peter L. Berger, and Thomas Luckmann, *The Social Construction of Reality: A Treatise in the Sociology of Knowledge*, New York 1966, p. 134, and Allen Lane The Penguin Press, London.

32. J. M. Keynes: *A Tract on Monetary Reform*, Macmillan, London, 1923, p. 45, reprinted in *Collected Writings* loc. cit., vol. IV, p. 36.

33. It is in this sense also that Simmel saw money as incorporating trust through the evolution of exchange. The merchant, he suggested, became the specialized and trusted bearer of the function of exchange which had previously taken place directly in the form of barter. As the merchant became the intermediary between exchanging individuals, so money came to stand between the objects of exchange. As the merchant embodied particular exchanges, so money embodies the process of exchange itself. (*Philosophie des Geldes*, op. cit., pp. 160–2.)

34. *Philosophie des Geldes*, op. cit., pp. 257–8.

NOTES TO CHAPTER IV

1. J. M. Keynes, *A Treatise on Money*, vol. I, p. 5, Macmillan, London 1935, and *Collected Writings*, op. cit., vol. V, p. 4 (italics added).

2. Charles Taylor, *Hegel*, loc. cit., p. 381 (italics added).

3. Dr. Lewis Thomas: "Language and Human Communication," *Dialogue*, Washington D.C., vol. 8, 1975, nos. 3–4, pp. 30–1.

He added. "Language, once it comes alive, behaves like an active, motile organism. Parts of it are always being changed, by a ceaseless activity to which all of us are committed."

4. Italics added.

5. *Rights and Right Conduct*, op. cit., pp. 13–16.

6. Ibid., p. 71.

7. Italics added.

8. A. I. Melden: "On Promising" in *Mind*, vol. 65 (New Series), January 1956, pp. 60–1.

9. H. L. A. Hart: "Are there any Natural Rights?", *The Philosophical Review*, vol. 64, 1955, p. 179, (italics added).

10. Ibid., p. 181.

11. Cf. Georg Friedrich Knapp: *Die Staatliche Theorie des Geldes*, 1905, 3rd ed. Munich and Leipzig 1921. A convenient summary of the essence of Knapp's nominalist theory, of which I have made use, will be found in Rist, loc. cit., pp. 353 ff. Cf. also the abbreviated English edition of Knapp's book *The State Theory of*

Money, abridged and translated by H. M. Lucas and James Bonar, London 1924.

12. Gail Pearson: "The Role of Money in Economic Growth", *Quarterly Journal of Economics*, p. 387, vol. 86, 1972.

13. Ibid. p. 387.

14. L. M. Lachmann: *The Legacy of Max Weber: Three Essays*, Heninemann, London 1970, p. 85.

15. Cf. pp. 10–11, above.

16. Cf. A paper read to the first Round Table Discussion of the International Economic Association in 1950 entitled "Some Aspects of International Economic Development of Under-developed Territories". Reprinted in *The Economic Impact on Under-developed Societies. Essays on International Investment and Social Change*, op. cit., p. 69.

17. Italics added. Rist (op. cit., p. 356) quotes the full "characteristic passage" from the English edition of Knapp's book p. 279 to which the above remarks refer, as follows:

It was not the gold standard per se that spread after 1871, but the English monetary system, which was the gold standard merely as it were by accident. In that case gold per se would be quite unimportant in the choosing of a standard. Was it only a question of historical circumstances, which were then (1875) favourable to gold? If the metallist puts this question, the chartalist can only answer Yes. All middle-sized and weaker States from exodromic considerations either have gone over to the gold standard or wish to do so. England is deaf to all suggestions of currency alterations, for she does not need to trouble herself with exodromic measures. It is the same with the system of military service. If the most victorious State has universal compulsory military service its neighbours must have it too in so far as they share the same battle-ground. England stands out of it because she does not join in the continental battles. If, however, European States want to enter on a world-wide policy (*Weltpolitik*), they must imitate England's navy; and, if England chooses to build ships of iron, her rivals must also choose the "iron standard" in shipbuilding.

18. The phrase is from James Bonar, (op. cit., p. 45).

19. This fallacious idea also failed to take into account the fact that the State or Government itself requires the money it receives in order to pay for the goods and services. The value of money will be influenced as much for the State as for private individuals by supply and demand factors and by what it will, or could be expected, to purchase at home and abroad.

20. Cf. Carl Menger's "Geld". Article in *Handwörterbuch der*

Staatswissenschaften, 3rd ed., vol. V, Jena 1909. (An earlier edition appeared in 1852.) Reprinted in *The Collected Works of Carl Menger*, vol. V, London School of Economics and Political Science Reprints, no. 20, 1936

21. Robert Giffen: "Fancy Monetary Standards", *Economic Journal*, vol. 2, 1892, p. 465. This article was introduced by the following passage: "It may be of some service to the study of questions of 'money' if I take the opportunity furnished by Mr. Aneurin Williams's paper on 'A Value of Bullion Standard' in the last issue of the *Economic Journal*, to refer students to a paper by Mr. Bagehot on what is substantially the same topic published in the *Economist* of November 20, 1875". (Also reprinted in the 1892 volume of the *Economist* at Giffen's suggestion.)

The article in question is entitled "A New Standard of Value", and is a criticism of Mr. Jevons's suggestion of a "multiple standard" in his book on "Money", in the International Scientific series which had just then appeared. Mr. Bagehot's article is anonymous, but of course it is well known that he was then the editor of the *Economist*, and I am in a position to state that the article was in fact his own writing. The subject is one in which he took a good deal of interest, as the article itself shows.

Mr. Williams's proposal of a "Value of Bullion Standard" and Mr. Jevons's of a "Multiple Standard" are not in all respects identical. Mr. Williams's proposal, as I understand it, is to provide for an issue of paper which is to consist of promises to pay a varying quantity of bullion, the variation to be made according to the average variation in the price of leading commodities arranged by an "index number". The paper thus issued is to constitute the "pounds" of the new system. Mr. Jevons's suggestion was that, while pounds are still to be so much bullion, the number of pounds payable for a debt was to be varied according to the variations of the "index number". In substance, it seems to me, the two proposals are so far identical. A promise to pay a varying quantity of bullion, the promise being regarded as the pound, and a promise to pay a varying number of sovereigns, which are still to be called pounds, appear to be much the same things, Mr. Bagehot's criticism applies alike to both proposals.

22. Italics added.

23. Cf. Milton Friedman, *Monetary Correction. A Proposal For Escalator Clauses To Reduce the Costs of Ending Inflation*, Occasional Paper no. 41, Institute of Economic Affairs, London 1974 (italics added).

NOTES TO CHAPTER V

1. Michael Oakeshott: *On Human Conduct*, Clarendon Press, Oxford 1975, p. 168.
2. Herr Schmidt, cf. *Financial Times*, London, 28 September 1972.
3. *Collected Writings*, vol. XV, p. 232, par. 74.
4. Ibid., par. 75, italics added.
5. Ibid.
6. Cf. Arthur Smithies: "Keynes Re-Visited", *Quarterly Journal of Economics*, vol. LXXXVI, no. 3, 1972, p. 463. Smithies was referring especially to Keynes's arguments in *Indian Currency and Finance* (*Collected Writings,* op. cit., vol. I). In this book Keynes took essentially the same position as in the Report of the Royal Commission on Indian Finance and Currency.
7. Paul Davidson: "A Keynesian View of Friedman's Theoretical Framework for Monetary Analysis", *Journal of Political Economy*, vol. 80, no. 5, September–October 1972, p. 871.
8. "The General Theory of Employment". An article by J. M. Keynes in *The Quarterly Journal of Economics*, February 1937, pp. 215–16.
9. Carl Menger had a more realistic view, as Erich Streissler has recently reminded us. He quotes the following passage from Menger's article "Geld": "The sums hoarded by private individuals, and partly even up to the present day by public authorities, have to be taken into account too, as they form part of the monetary requirements of a people during certain periods, in spite of the fact that they are by definition not used in payment during the period in question." (The article is in *Ein Handwörterbuch der Staatswissenschaften*, first to third edn. 1891–1909 quoted from *The Collected Works of Carl Menger* (F. A. Hayek, ed.), vol. IV, London 1936, p. 109 (Streissler's translation).

Streissler goes on to point out that Menger: "tried to create a brand of monetary theory under uncertainty, basically a disequilibrium theory of money . . . he does not evisage money as something whose use is precisely planned by much rather as a buffer stock against the non-fulfillment of plans".

(Erich W. Streissler: "Menger's Theories of Money and Uncertainty – A Modern Interpretation", in J. R. Hicks and W. Weber,

Editors, *Carl Menger and the Austrian School of Economics*, Clarendon Press, Oxford 1973.)

10. In contrast to the uncertainty existing in the real world, Davidson rightly makes the point that

All Walrasian general equilibrium models *imply* worlds of certainty. The *tâtonnement* process, which is essential to the establishment of equilibrium and implies no transactions occur until equilibrium is attained (that is, recontracting is essential), implies that anyone holding money either at any point in the auction or till the next market period is demented or at least economically irrational. Why hold money if it is not needed for transactions, since in equilibrium goods trade for goods, and since the present and future values of all economic goods can be determined, at least in a probability sense, with complete certainty? The essential nature of money is disregarded in the Walrasian system, as no asset exists whose liquidity premium always exceeds its carrying costs.

(Davidson 1969, p. 319). He quotes Hahn as saying, *"The Walrasian economy* that we have been considering, although one where the auctioneer regulates the terms at which goods shall exchange, *is essentially one of barter."* (Italics added).The point, however, is, I suggest, that what Keynes was trying to find was not a Walrasian auctioneer but a Super-Walrasian Calculator somehow able to *remove* uncertainty by a new kind of collective wisdom. I deal with this point again later.

11. G. L. S. Shackle "Keynes and Today's Establishment in Economic Theory: A View", *Journal of Economic Literature*, June 1973, vol. XI, number 2, p. 516 (italics added).

12. Shackle is referring in particular to the book by Axel Leijonhufvud, *On Keynesian Economics and the Economics of Keynes. A Study in Monetary Theory*, New York, London and Toronto, Oxford University Press 1968.

13. Electronic Random Number Indicating Equipment.

14. *Collected Papers*, op. cit., vol. IX, p. 272. This essay was first published in 1926.

15. Italics added.

16. Italics added. Keynes continued (ibid., p. 292), "Yes it would leave private initiative and enterprise unhindered. Even if these measures prove insufficient, nevertheless they will furnish us with better knowledge than we have now for taking the next step."

17. Shackle, op. cit., p. 518.

18. Cf. Karl R. Popper: *Objective Knowledge, An Evolutionary*

Approach, Oxford, Clarendon Press 1972, pp. 341–2. He added: "Bacon speaks of perceptions as 'grapes, ripe and in season' which have to be gathered, patiently and industriously and from which, if pressed, the pure wine of knowledge will flow."

19. Italics added. F. A. Hayek has pointed out in *Law, Legislation and Liberty*, vol. I, University of Chicago Press, 1973 that "the refusal to recognize as binding any rules of conduct whose justification had not been rationally demonstrated ... becomes in the nineteenth century an ever recurring theme".

Hayek adds:

The best description of this state of mind by a representative thinker of our time is found in the account given by Lord Keynes in a talk entitled "My early beliefs". Speaking in 1938 about the time thirty-five years before, when he himself was twenty, he says of himself and his friends: We entirely repudiated a personal liability on us to obey general rules. "We claimed the right to judge every individual case on its merits, and the wisdom, experience, and self-control to do so successfully. This was a very important part of our faith, violently and aggressively held, and for the outer world it was our most obvious and dangerous characteristic. We repudiated entirely customary morals, conventions, and traditional wisdom. We were, that is to say, in the strict sense of the term, immoralists ... we recognized no moral obligation, no inner sanction, to conform or obey. Before heaven we claimed to be our own judge in our own case."

To which he added: "So far as I am concerned, it is too late to change. I remain, and always will remain, an immoralist."

To anyone who has himself grown up before the First World War, it is obvious that this was then not an attitude peculiar to the Bloomsbury Group, but a very widespread one, shared by many of the most active and independent spirits of the time. (Quoted from John Maynard Keynes: *Two Memoirs*, London 1949, p. 97.)

For a detailed treatment of the influence of the Bloomsbury Group on J. M. Keynes see Helen Phillips: *J. M. Keynes – Vision and Technique*, Stanford Honours Essays in Humanities, no. I, Stanford University Press 1952.

20. Cf. Elizabeth Johnson, loc. cit. Quoted by her from "The Commemoration of Thomas Robert Malthus. The Allocutions III. Mr. Keynes", *Economic Journal*, June 1935. Reprinted in *Essays in Biography* in *Collected Writings of J. M. Keynes*, vol. X (italics added).

21. In the Preface to *The Economic Consequences of the Peace* (published by Macmillan, London in 1919) Keynes wrote:

The writer of this book was temporarily attached to the British Treasury during the war and was their official representative at the Paris Peace Conference; he also sat as deputy for the Chancellor of the Exchequer on the Supreme Economic Council, up to 7 June 1919. He resigned from these positions when it became finally evident that hope could no longer be entertained of substantial modification in the draft Terms of Peace. The grounds of his objection to the Treaty, or rather to the whole policy of the conference towards the economic problems of Europe, will appear in the following chapters. (Reprinted in the _Collected Writings_ in vol. II.)

22. Joseph A. Schumpeter, in _The New Economics_ ed. Seymour E. Harris, New York, Alfred A. Knopf, 1947, p. 80, quoted by Helen Philips, op. cit., p. 8. He added: "Here we have the origin of the modern stagnation thesis. . . . Every comprehensive "theory" . . . of an economic state of society consists of two complementary but essentially distinct elements. There is, first, the theorist's view about the basic features of that state of society, about what is and what is not important in order to understand its life at a given time. Let us call this his vision. And there is, second, the theorist's technique, an apparatus by which he conceptualizes his vision and which turns the latter into concrete propositions or 'theories'.

23. Italics added.
24. Cf. L. M. Lachmann: _The Legacy of Max Weber_, op. cit., pp. 70–2.
25. _Collected Writings_, vol. II, p. 6.
26. Ibid., p. 9, 10 and 11. Italics added.
27. Ibid., p. 11. Keynes was fond of referring to psychological factors but as various writers have pointed out, in particular Professor Gunter Schmölders, his psychology was of the crudest. It consisted largely in setting up abstract puppets or models of his own very unsophisticated beliefs concerning the motives which cause individuals to act in a certain manner. (Cf. Gunter Schmölders: "J. M. Keynes's Beitrag zur ökonomischen Verhaltensforschung" in G. Schmölders, R. Schröder, H. St. Seidenfus, _John Maynard Keynes als "Psychologe"_, Duncker und Humblot, Berlin 1956, pp. 7–24.)
28. Italics added.
29. Cf. J. A. Schumpeter in Seymour E. Harris, op. cit., p. 80.
30. _Essays in Biography_, p. 4, _Collected Writings_, op. cit., vol. X.
31. Ibid., p. 11.
32. Ibid., p. 12.
33. Italics added.

34. Ibid., p. 13 (italics added).
35. "Lenin" he wrote

is said to have declared that the best way to destroy the capitalist system was to debauch the currency. By a continuing process of inflation, governments can confiscate, secretly and unobserved, an important part of the wealth of their citizens. By this method they not only confiscate, but they confiscate *arbitrarily*; and, while the process impoverishes many, it actually enriches some. The sight of this arbitrary rearrangement of riches strikes not only at security, but at confidence in the equity of the existing distribution of wealth. .... As the inflation proceeds and the real value of the currency fluctuates wildly from month to month, all permanent relations between debtors and creditors, which form the ultimate foundation of capitalism, become so utterly disordered as to be almost meaningless; and the process of wealth-getting degenerates into a gamble and a lottery. Lenin was certainly right. There is no subtler, no surer means of overturning the existing basis of society than to debauch the currency. The process engages all the hidden forces of economic law on the side of destruction, and does it in a manner which not one man in a million is able to diagnose. (*Collected Writings*, vol. II, p. 149).

36. Ibid., p. 150.
37. Ibid., p. 150.
38. *Journal of Political Economy*, vol. 80, no. 5, p. 908. The hypothesis, namely, "that a highly unstable marginal efficiency schedule of investment and a liquidity preference function that is highly elastic at low rates of interest and unstable at higher rates of interest are the key to short-run economic movements. That is what gives investment its central role, what makes the consumption function and the multiplier the key concepts, what enables Keynes to develop his theory for 165 pages without having to introduce the quantity of money."
39. Italics added.
40. Quoted from *Essays in Persuasion* in Keynes: *Collected Writings*, op. cit., vol. IX, by Elizabeth Johnson: "John Maynard Keynes: Scientist or Politician?", *Journal of Political Economy*, 1974, p. 105.
41. *Collected Writings*, op. cit., vol. VII, p. 267
42. Italics added.
43. Ibid., p. 164 (italics added).
44. William Breit and Roger L. Ransom: *The Academic Scribblers – American Economists in Collision*. Holt, Rinehart & Winston, Inc., New York 1967, p. 208.

45. *Collected Writings*, op. cit., vol. VII, p. xxvi.

46. "A Short View of Russia" written in 1925, published in *Essays in Persuasion*, Macmillan, 1931, and *Collected Writings*, vol. IX, p. 268.

47. *Collected Writings*, vol. IX, pp. 268–9.

48. Of course, Keynes was fully aware of the less attractive aspects of the Russia he was considering and the mood of oppression there. But he commented: "In part, no doubt, it is the fruit of Red revolution – there is much in Russia to make one pray that one's own country may achieve its goal not in that way." Yet true to the irrational prejudices of the past, and the radical excesses of the nineteen-thirties, he added: "In part, perhaps, it is the fruit of some beastliness in the Russian nature – or in the Russian and Jewish natures when, as now, they are allied together. But in part it is one face of the superb earnestness of Red Russia, of the high serious-ness, which in its other aspect appears as the spirit of elation" (ibid. p. 270).

49. Ibid., p. 259. Is this phrase just accidential? I think not. This is not the only passage in which Keynes contrasts the idea of absolute moral standards with what he regards as the need for a monetary system not based on traditional morality.

50. From chapter V: "The Money Motive" in *Laissez-faire and Communism*, p. 74, New Republic. Inc., New York 1926. Reprinted in vol. X, *Collected Writings*, op. cit., p. 293.

51. Cf. Dudley Dillard: "The Theory of a Monetary Economy". Chapter I in *Post-Keynesian Economics*, ed. by Kenneth K. Kuri-hara, Rutgers University Press, 1954, and George Allen & Unwin, London 1955.

52. Keynes's essay appeared in the *Festschrift* under the title "Der stand und die nächste Zukunft der Konjunkturforschung" Munich, Duncker und Humblot, 1933.

53. Dillard op. cit., pp. 18–19.

54. *General Theory, Collected Writings*, op. cit., vol. VII, p. 294.

55. Ibid., p. 241.

56. Ibid., p. 287. Keynes was here referring to Alfred Marshall's well-known description of the business class in "The Social Pos-sibilities of Economic Chivalry", *Economic Journal*, 1907, vol. XVII, p. 9. The relevant passage is on pp. 286–7, *Collected Writings*, vol. IX.

57. Quoted by McCulloch in his *Principles of Political Economy*.

58. *Collected Writings,* vol. IX, p. 288.

59. For the original context in which these words were used see p. 66 above.

60. Cf. John Rawls: *A Theory of Justice,* Clarendon Press, Oxford 1971, p. 547.

61. *The General Theory, Collected Writings,* vol. VII, op. cit., p. 156.

62. Cf. S. Herbert Frankel: *Investment and the Return to Equity Capital in the South African Gold Mining Industry 1887–1965. An International Comparison,* Basil Blackwell, Oxford 1967, and Harvard University Press, p. 48. I concluded in this study that it indicated:

how effectively the private international capital market operated in a highly risky field of investment. It also shows how misleading it is to attempt to assess the benefits of investment only over short periods of time. Investment is a continuing and long-term activity, and risk-bearing is a co-operant process involving the sharing of risks over different time periods, in different circumstances, and by investors resident in different countries.

63. *The General Theory, Collected Writings,* op. cit., vol. VII, p. 160.

64. See also Günter Schmölders: "Von der 'Quantitätstheorie' zur 'Liquiditätstheorie' des Geldes". *Abhandlungen der Geistes – und Sozialwissenschaftlichen Klasse Jahrgang 1960,* nr. 12, Verlag der Akademie der Wissenschaften und der Literatur in Mainz in Kommission bei Franz Steiner Verlag GMBH, Wiesbaden.

65. *The General Theory, Collected Writings,* op. cit., vol. VII, p. 160.

66. Paul M. Sweezy some years ago referred to

Keynes's habit of treating the State as a *deus ex machina* to be invoked whenever his human actors, behaving according to the rules of the capitalist game, get themselves into a dilemma from which there is apparently no escape. Naturally, this Olympian interventionist resolves everything in a manner satisfactory to the author and presumably to the audience. The only trouble is – as every Marxist knows – that the State is not a god but one of the actors who has a part to play just like all the other actors.

Cf. "Keynes, The Economist" (3), chap. X, p. 108, in *The New Economics. Keynes' Influence on Theory and Public Policy,* ed. by Seymour E. Harris (Dennis Dobson, London 1960). The only trouble is, unfortunately, that this non-omniscience of the State has not been generally recognized by authoritarian regimes – or, indeed, by those who wish to use monetary policy as an instrument of the State.

67. Ibid., *Collected Writings*, vol. VII, p. 160, (italics added).

68. Reprinted in *Collected Writings*, op. cit., vol. IV, p. 59.

69. This is well illustrated by the typical psychologizing in the following passage (ibid, p. 161, *General Theory*).

Even apart from the instability due to speculation, there is the instability due to the characteristic of human nature that a large proportion of our positive activities depend on spontaneous optimism rather than on a mathematical expectation, whether moral or hedonistic or economic. Most, probably, of our decisions to do something positive, the full consequences of which will be drawn out over many days to come, can only be taken as a result of animal spirits – of a spontaneous urge to action rather than inaction, and not as the outcome of a weighted average of quantitative benefits multiplied by quantitative probabilities. . . .

70. The idea of the "irrationality" of individual calculation from the point of view of society was the subject of a large literature to some of which Keynes himself referred (e.g. to Silvio Gesell). This literature regarded it as highly irrational to entertain the optimistic belief that somehow *private* monetary calculation could further the general good. An example is an article by Arthur Salz. It claimed to trace the "irrational belief" in a beneficent economic order, based on private enterprise and *laissez-faire*, to Ricardo and Adam Smith. The idea expressed by Salz is that the very concept of the economic rationality of the entrepreneur or businessman is itself irrational. The much-vaunted rationality of business enterprise is simply the exercise of reason in a social setting in which society has so organized the conditions of enterprise that the businessman in following the profit motive is able to succeed. He does so, not because he necessarily acts rationally in the interests of the whole society, but simply because he acts rationally in his own protected situation. (Cf. "Die Irrationale Grundlage der Kapitalistischen Wirtschaft und Gesellschaftsordnung", in *Sociologische Studien Alfred Weber Gewidmet*, Heidelberg 1930.)

71. In the article, to which I have previously referred, explaining parts of his own book, *The General Theory* he wrote: "The whole object of the accumulation of *Wealth* is to produce results, or potential results, at a comparatively distant, and sometimes at an *indefinitely* distant, date. Thus the fact that our knowledge of the future is fluctuating, vague, and uncertain, renders *Wealth* a peculiarly

unsuitable subject for the methods of the classical economic theory." "The General Theory of Employment", *Quarterly Journal of Economics,* February 1937, p. 213.

72. Italics added.

73. Keynes is implying that what appears rational to the capitalist actors is but a partial rationality. They are busy playing a game: the rules of which they understand. These rules are, allegedly, made *in their interests* by the State. The actors continue to believe that they are playing the game in the interests of society as a whole, even when the game breaks down. This happens in periods of depression and unemployment. Keynes therefore assumes the necessity to bring into play another agent who will stand above, and be able to look beyond, the activities of the little business actors ensconced in their illusory cocoon. This other agent is, as we have already seen, none other than the State – of which, however, Keynes had a most esoteric conception. He expressed this as follows: "The next step forward must come, not from political agitation or premature experiments, *but from thought. We need an effort of the mind to elucidate our own feelings.* At present our sympathy and our judgement are liable to be on different sides, which is a painful and paralysing state of mind. In the field of action reformers will not be successful until they can *steadily pursue a clear and definite object with their intellects and their feelings in tune"* (italics added). Years later this view is still being quoted and echoed by Professor Joan Robinson in "The Final of Laissez-faire" (vol. 3, *Collected Economic Papers*, p. 145). Having argued that *laissez-faire* ideology is no longer appropriate she still could find no way out of the resulting impasse. She wrote:

> All the same, the disintegration of the old creed leaves a gap. What is it all supposed to be for? Political aims require economic planning to carry them out. It is equally true that economic planning requires political aims. Without some aim, how are the planners to know what to plan? The new cry for growth . . . is not an aim in itself. What is to grow? . . . Even the mild degree of planning represented by government intervention to assist the great firms to co-ordinate their activities brings economic questions into the arena of democratic politics, from which the doctrine of *laissez-faire* was designed to fence them off.

74. In *Festschrift für Arthur Spiethoff*, loc. cit., p. 124.

75. In his *Theory of Social and Economic Organization*, London 1947, p. 170, Weber wrote "the term 'formal rationality of

economic action will be used to designate the extent of quantitative calculation or accounting which is technically possible and which is actually applied". He added:

A system of economic activity will be called "formally" rational according to the degree in which the provision for needs which is essential to every rational economy, is capable of being expressed in *numerical, calculable terms, and is so expressed.* [But] *it is not sufficient to consider only the purely formal fact that calculations are being made on grounds of expediency by the methods which are, among those available, technically the most nearly adequate.* In addition it is necessary to take account of the fact that economic activity is oriented to ultimate ends (Forderungen) of some kind whether they be ethical, political, utilitarian, hedonistic, the attainment of social distinction, of social equality or of anything else. *Substantive rationality cannot be measured in terms of formal calculation alone, but also involves a relation to the absolute values or to the content of the particular given ends to which it is oriented.* In principle, there is an indefinite number of possible standards of value which are "rational" in this issue. Socialistic and communistic standards which, though by no means unambiguous in themselves, always involve elements of social justice and equality form only one group among the indefinite plurality of possible points of view. . . In addition, it is possible to criticize the attitude towards the economic activity itself or towards the mean used, from ethical, ascetic points of view. Of all these the merely formal calculation in money terms may seem either of quite secondary importance or even as *fundamentally evil in itself,* quite apart from the consequences of the modern methods of calculation.

(All quotations are from the translation of *Wirtschaft und Gesellschaft,* Part 1, 1947 Edition, edited by A. R. Henderson and Talcott Parsons (italics added)).

76. David Beetham: *Max Weber and the Theory of Modern Politics,* pp. 274–5, George Allen & Unwin Ltd, London 1974.

77. Beetham writes in this connection:

. . . Weber believed that modern capitalism was in fact substantively rational also, from the standpoint both of the production of goods and the satisfaction of wants. If the standard used is that of the provision of a certain minimum of subsistence for the maximum size of population, the experience of the last few decades would seem to show that formal and substantive rationality coincide to a relatively high degree. Equally, however, formal and substantive rationality could conflict, as in a socialist planned economy, which would produce an "inevitable reduction in the formal rationality of calculation" and hence of productive efficiency.

Ibid., p. 274.

78. Weber himself seems to have been bothered by this problem without being able to disentangle it. Beetham points out that Weber insisted that he was using the concept of rationality:

in a purely formal, technical sense, and that this implied no evaluation from any substantive viewpoint. Indeed, in his political writings and in other areas (e.g. bureaucracy and science), Weber showed himself to be critical of the extension of formal rationality as an end in itself. Nevertheless, such a criticism could only be made from a substantive value standpoint and thus could not form the subject of science, since there were "an indefinite number of positive standards of value which are 'rational' in this sense". There could be no question of making a judgement from such a standpoint in a scientific work.

Ibid., p. 274.

79. S. Herbert Frankel: *The Economic Impact on Under-Developed Societies. Essays on International Investment and Social Change* (see the essay, "Intercomparability of National Income Aggregates", op. cit., p. 41).

NOTES TO CHAPTER VI

1. G. Warren Nutter: "Freedom In A Revolutionary Economy", in *The American Revolution: Three Views*, American Brands, Inc., New York 1975.
2. R. A. Lehfeldt: *Restoration of the World's Currencies*, P. S. King & Son Ltd, London 1923.
3. Cf. Hayek: *Law, Legislation and Liberty*. op. cit., p. 32. He added:

The illusion that reason alone can tell us what we ought to do, and that therefore all reasonable men ought to be able to join in the endeavour to pursue common ends as members of an organization, is quickly dispelled when we attempt to put it into practice. But the desire to use our reason to turn the whole of society into one rationally directed engine persists, and in order to realize it common ends are imposed upon all that cannot be justified by reason and cannot be more than the decisions of particular wills.

4. Peters, op. cit., p. 152.
5. In Hector-Neri Castañeda and George Nakhnikian (Eds.): *Morality and the Language of Conduct*, Wayne State University Press, Detroit 1963.
6. Cf. Editor's Preface, ibid., p. viii.

7. Art Buchwald: "My Fellow Americans", *Washington Post*, Washington D.C. Reprinted in *Daily Progress*, Charlottesville, Virginia, 29 May 1972.

8. As J. Glenn Gray has recently reminded us in: "Hegel's Logic: The Philosophy of the Concrete", *The Virginia Quarterly Review*, vol. 47, no. 2, Spring 1971, pp. 185 ff.

Normally we mean by anything concrete that which is particular and perceivable by the senses, and by abstract we mean what is non-sensible, without time-space existence. This table is concrete and that student to whom I am responding. If I were to speak about the form of all tables, tableness, or about man rather than that student over there, I would be talking abstractly. In the realm of thinking, however, particularly philosophical thought, Hegel teaches us that the situation is different. There the concrete is the many-sided, the complex, and contextual – anything seen in all its relationships together with its origins and ends. Hegel takes the word concrete in its etymological sense of *concrescere* – to grow together. The abstract, on the other hand, from *abstrahere* – to draw out from – is anything seen apart from its relations and context in a living whole. For example, a history of art, studied without reference to a people's religion, economic system, political institutions, et cetera, would be abstract. It might be desirable, of course, to study art history in this way, but one would not understand the whole truth of art unless one understands it as an organic expression of a people's entire way of grasping their world. The same can be said of any other single discipline. The true is the whole and the whole truth is the concrete.

To illustrate the difference between the concrete and the abstract he refers to Hegel's example of:

the case of a young man who has murdered someone being led to the gallows in the presence of the populace. [Hegel's time was almost as terrible as our own!] Perhaps some ladies remark on how strong, handsome, and interesting he looks and meet with indignation on the part of the uninformed multitude. How could a murderer be handsome or interesting? This is abstract thinking [Hegel writes], to see nothing in the murderer except the abstract fact that he is a murderer, and to annul all other human essence in him with this simple quality.

9. Peter L. Berger, Brigitte Berger and Hansfried Kellner: *The Homeless Mind*, p. 167, Penguin Books, 1974, Harmondsworth, England; Random House, U.S.A.

10. Martin Bronfenbrenner: "Some Neglected Implications of Secular Inflation", in *Post-Keynesian Economics*, ed. K. K. Kurihara, Rutgers University Press, 1954. Quoted by G. L. Bach: *The*

New Inflation, Causes, Effects, Cures, Prentice-Hall, Inc., Englewood Cliffs, N.J., 1972, p. 62. Bach suggests that

part of this income transfer has taken place during the inflation of the past two decades. The profit share of the national income has been squeezed substantially, although that of interest and rent has risen somewhat. . . . Perhaps the effective real rate of return on investment is already so low that sufficient new private investment cannot be counted on to maintain healthy economic growth; some conservatives argue that this is the case. Perhaps the rate could drop much further than Bronfenbrenner suggested; some liberals and labor leaders argue that the danger point is far removed. But whether the danger point is near or far, to pretend that it will never be reached is merely to avoid facing what may sooner or later become a real problem for the capitalist economy of the United States.

11. Helmut Schoeck: *Envy: A Theory of Social Behaviour*, Secker & Warburg, London 1969, p. 298. See also his discussion on p. 306 of the views of E. J. Mishan in "A Survey of Welfare Economics, 1939–1959", *The Economic Journal*, London, vol. LXX, p. 247, June 1960, and of J. S. Duesenberry's *Income, Saving, and the Theory of Consumer Behavior*, Cambridge, Mass. 1949. Schoeck writes:

In this view, the subjective sense of well-being of every income group is prejudiced by the income groups above it. In order to be rid of this "feeling of deprivation" recourse is had to the progressive income tax. Mishan then writes:

Ideally, of course, the tax should suffice to cover all the initial and subsequent claims necessary to *placate* everybody in the lower-income groups, and the stronger is this envy of others, the heavier must be the tax.

Mishan continues, that according to Duesenberry, who speaks for many like-minded people, there can be a situation of "excessive" income in which "any net increase of output – for instance, more of "every" good without additional effort – will not advance the welfare of the community no matter how it is distributed. *Indeed, any increase of output makes the community worse off, since, no matter how the additional goods are distributed, the additional envy generated cannot be adequately compensated for out of these extra goods.*

Mishan. . . is, however, critical of this view. In his opinion, there might be a distribution of additional goods, made available without any additional effort, which, in spite of evident envy, would improve the position of everyone in the society. Yet . . . *it is envy's nature to be on principle wholly intractable to quantitative manipulations.* . . . (italics added).

12. William Fellner: "The Dollar's Place in the International Sys-

tem", *Journal of Economic Literature*, September 1972, vol. X, pp. 735 ff.

13. G. L. Bach: "The Economic Effects of Inflation: Long-term Problems", *Proceedings of the Academy of Political Science*, vol. 31. no. 4, 1975, p. 26.

Net Debtor or Creditor Status of Major Economic Sectors, 1939–72
(in billions of dollars)

	1939	1949	1960	1972
Households	+87	+249	+337	+856
Unincorporated business	+3	+16	−21	−115
Nonfinancial corporations	−25	−17	−67	−228
Financial corporations	−3	+17	+32	−130
Governments	−68	−263	−251	−399

Source: Data for 1939 from Raymond Goldsmith, *A Study of Saving in the United States*, vol. 3, tables W-14, 15, 16 (Princeton: Princeton University Press, 1955); data for other years from Federal Reserve flow-of-funds accounts.

Note: + indicates net creditor status, − indicates net debtor status.

14. Unanticipated inflation also brought about a massive transfer of wealth from the elderly to the young, who went heavily into debt to set up households, buy cars, furniture and the like. As the elderly had relatively few debts they were more vulnerable to inflation because more of their assets were in monetary form (cf. Bach, ibid., p. 28).

15. On this see Fernand Braudel: *Capitalism and Material Life*, op. cit., chap. 7.

16. I use this word as expressing, in a general sense, a similar notion to that contained in Hegel's use of the word *Sittlichkeit*, to which I have previously referred, and to Simmel's idea of *Vornehmheit* as a condition of monetary order. I have recently found that Michael Oakeshott uses it to mean "the civil condition or civil relationship". This he calls "an ideal character". He writes: "The civil condition . . . is not an association of ascertainable persons identifiable in respect of a place and a time, by the signs it uses to recognise itself, or specifiable in terms of common beliefs or of its own rules and arrangements. *It is a certain mode of association*, one among others. . . . I shall call it the relationship of civility". (Italics added.) Oakeshott, op. cit., pp. 108 and 118–84.

NOTES TO APPENDIX

1. Spykman, op. cit., p. xxvi.
2. Donald N. Levine: *Georg Simmel on Individuality and Social Forms*, The University of Chicago Press, Chicago and London 1971, p. xii.

Bibliography

Acton, H. B., *The Illusion of the Epoch. Marxism-Leninism as a Philosophical Creed.* Cohen & West Ltd., London 1955.

Altman, S. P., Review Article of Georg Simmel's "Die Philosophie Des Geldes", *American Journal of Sociology*, 1903.

Avineri, Shlomo., *The Social and Political Thought of Karl Marx.* Cambridge University Press 1968.

Bach, G. L., "The Economic Effects of Inflation: Long Term Problems", *Proceedings of the Academy of Political Science*, vol. 31, no. 4, 1975.

Bach, G. L., *The New Inflation Causes Effects Cures.* Prentice-Hall, Englewood Cliffs, N. J. 1972.

Becher James F., "The Corporation Spirit and its Liberal Analysis", *Journal of the History of Ideas,* vol. XXX, January/June 1969.

Beetham, David, *Max Weber and The Theory of Modern Politics.* George Allen & Unwin Ltd, London 1974.

Bendix Reinhard, *Embattled Reason.* New York 1970.

Bagehot, Walter, *Lombard Street: A Description of the Money Market.* London 1873.

Berger, Peter L. and Brigitte, and Kellner H., *The Homeless Mind Modernization and Consciousness.* Pelican Books 1974 and Random House 1973.

Berger, Peter L., and Luckmann, Thomas, *The Social Construction of Reality: A Treatise in the Sociology of Knowledge.* New York 1966.

Berlin, Sir Isaiah, *The Life and Opinions of Moses Hess.* W. Heffer & Sons Ltd, Cambridge 1959.

Bonar James, *Philosophy and Political Economy in some of their Historical Relations.* London 1893.

Bongie, Laurence L., *David Hume Prophet of the Counter-Revolution*. Clarendon Press, Oxford 1965.

Boulding, Kenneth E., *Essays on Society, Religion and Ethics: Toward a General Theory of Growth*. Ann Arbor 1968.

Braudel, Fernand, *Capitalism and Material Life 1400–1800*. Translated by Miriam Kochan. Weidenfeld and Nicolson, London 1973.

Breit, William and Ransom, Roger L., *The Academic Scribblers: American Economists in Collision*. Holt Rinehart and Winston, New York 1967.

Bronfenbrenner, Martin, *Some Neglected Implications of Secular Inflation in Post-Keynesian Economics*. K. Kurihara ed., Rutgers University Press, New Brunswick, N. J. 1954.

Brunner, Karl, "A Survey of Selected Issues in Monetary Theory", *Schweizerische Zeitschrift für Volkswirtschaft und Statistik*, no. 1, 1971, pp. 1–146.

Buchanan, James M., *Cost and Choice: an Inquiry in Economic Theory*. Markham Publishing Co., Chicago 1969.

Buchanan, James M., *The Limits of Liberty between Anarchy and Leviathan*. The University of Chicago Press, Chicago 1975.

Burke, Edmund, *Works*. Rivington Edition, London 1826–7.

Busschau, W. J., *The Measure of Gold the Role of God as International Money*. Central News Agency Ltd. South Africa 1949.

Cantillon, Higgs Henry, ed., *Essai sur la nature du commerce*.

Castañeda, Hector-Neri and Nakhunikian George, eds, *Morality and the Language of Conduct*. Wayne State University Press, Detroit 1963.

Castañeda, Hector-Neri, "Thinking and Doing. The Philosophical Foundations of Institutions", *Philosophical Studies Series in Philosophy*, vol. 7, D. Reidel Publishing Co., Dordrecht, Holland and Boston, U.S.A. 1975.

Cavell, Stanley, "The Avoidance of Love. A Reading of King Lear" in *Must We Mean What We Say?*, Charles Scribner's Sons, New York 1969.

Cecco, Marcello de, *Money and Empire, The International Gold Standard, 1890–1914*. Basil Blackwell, Oxford 1974.

Clower, R., "Is there an Optimal Money Supply?", *Journal of Finance*, May 1970, vol. 25, pp. 425–33.

Cohn, Arthur Wolfgang, *Kann das Geld abgeschaft werden?* Gustav Fisher, Jena 1920.

Daniels, Norman, ed., *Reading Rawls: Critical Studies of A Theory of Justice*. Blackwell, Oxford 1975.

David, Felix, "Profit Inflation and Industrial Growth", *Quarterly Journal of Economics*, LXX, 1956, pp. 441–63.

Davidson, Paul, "A Keynesian View of Friedman's Theoretical Framework for Monetary Analysis", *Journal of Political Economy*, vol. 80, no. 5, September/October 1972.

Demsetz, H., "The Cost of Transacting", *Quarterly Journal of Economics*, February 1968.

Dillard, Dudley, "The Theory of a Monetary Economy", Kurihara K., ed., *Post-Keynesian Economics*. Rutgers University Press 1954 and George Allen & Unwin, London 1955.

Duncan G., *Marx and Mill: Two Views of Social Conflict and Social Harmony*. Cambridge University Press 1973.

Einzig, P., *Primitive Money in its Ethnological Historical and Economical Aspects*. London 1949.

Ellis, Howard S., *German Monetary Theory*. Harvard University Press 1934.

Fellner, William, "The Dollar's Place in the International System", *Journal of Economic Literature*, vol. X, September 1972.

Fetter, Frank A., *Economic Principles*. The Century Co., New York 1915.

Fetter, Frank A., "Interest Theories Old and New", *American Review*, March 1914, pp. 68–92.

Firth, R., "Ethical Absolutism and the ideal Observer", *Philosophy and Phenomenological Research Quarterly Journal*, vol. XII, no. 3, March 1952.

Flemming, J. Marcus, "Towards a New Regime for International Payments", *Journal of International Economics*, vol. 2, no. 4, September 1972.

Flemming, John, *Inflation*. Oxford University Press 1976.

Frankel, S. Herbert, *The Economic Impact on Under-Developed Societies Essays on International Investment and Social Change*. Basil Blackwell, Oxford 1953.

Frankel, S. Herbert, *Investment and the Return to Equity Capital in the South African Gold Mining Industry 1887–1965: An International Comparison*. Basil Blackwell, Oxford, and Harvard University Press 1967.

Friedman, Milton, "The Role of Monetary Policy", *American Economic Review*, vol. LVIII, no. 1, March 1968.

Friedman, Milton, "The Optimum Quantity of Money", in M. Friedman, ed., *The Optimum Quantity of Money and Other Essays*. Chicago 1969.

Friedman, Milton, *Some Theoretical and Empirical Results*. Occasional Paper 68, National Bureau of Economic Research Inc. 1959.

Friedman, Milton, *Monetary Correction*. Occasional Paper 41, Institute of Economic Affairs 1974.

Friedman, Milton, "Money: Quantity Theory", *International Encyclopaedia of the Social Sciences*. 1968.

Friedman, Milton, "The Quantity Theory of Money A Restatement", in M. Friedman, ed., *Studies in the Quantity Theory of Money*. Chicago 1956.

Friedman, Milton, *Capitalism and Freedom*. Chicago 1962.

Friedman, Milton, *A Programme for Monetary Stability*. Fordham University Press, New York 1960.

Friedrich, Karl J., "Rational Decision". In *Nomos* JA 37.

Fritsch, B., *Die Geld und Kredittheorie von Karl Marx*. Zürich 1934.

Gaettens, B., *Inflation – Das Drama der Geldentwertung vom Aktertum bis zur Gegenwart*. München 1955.

Gassen, K., and Landmann M., eds., *Buch Des Dankes an Georg Simmel*. 1958.

Gerloff, W., *Die Entstehung des Geldes und die Anfänge des Geldwesens*. Frankfurt A. M. 1947.

Gerloff, W., *Gesellschaftliche Theorie des Geldes*. Innsbruck 1950.

Giddens, Anthony, *Capitalism and Modern Social Theory*.

Ginsberg, Morris, *Reason and Unreason in Society: Essays in Sociology and Social Philosophy*. 1947.

Gilbert, J. C., "The Demand for Money: The Development of an Economic Concept", *Journal of Political Economy*, April 1953, pp. 144–59.

Graham, Frank D., "Partial Reserve Money and the 100 per cent Proposal", *American Economic Review*, September 1936, p. 436.

Gray, J. Glen, "Hegel's Logic: The Philosophy of the Concrete", *The Virginia Quarterly Review*, vol. 47, no. 2, Spring 1971.

Groseclose, Elgin, *Fifty years of Managed Money. The Story of the Federal Reserve, 1913–1963*. Macmillan & Co. Ltd., London.

Grossman, Herschel I., "Was Keynes A. Keynesian?", *Journal of Economic Literature*, vol. X, no. 1, March 1972.

Haber, Franz, *Untersuchungen Über Irrtümer Moderner Geldverbesserer*. Jena 1926.

Haberler, Gottfried, *Money in the International Economy*. Hobart Paper 31, The Institute of Economic Affairs, London 1965.

Haberler, Gottfried, *The Challenge to the Free Market Economy*. American Enterprise Institute, 1975.

Haberler, Gottfried, *The World Economy, Money and the Great Depression 1919–1939*. American Enterprise Institute 1976.

Harris, Seymour E., *The Assignats*. Harvard University Press 1930.

Harris, Seymour E., ed. and with Introduction, *The New Economics, Keynes' Influence on Theory and Public Policy*. Dennis Dobson Ltd, London 1947.

Hart, H. L. A., "Are There Natural Rights?", *The Philosophical Review*, vol. 64, 1955.

Hartley, R. E., "Importance and Nature of Communication", in Steinberg C. S., ed., *Mass Media and Communication*. New York, 1966.

Hayek, Friedrich, ed., *Beiträge zur Geld Theorie*. 1933.

Hayek, F. A., *Monetary Nationalism and International Stability*. The Graduate School of International Studies, Geneva 1937.

Hayek, F. A., *The Constitution of Liberty*. Routledge & Kegan Paul, London, and Chicago 1960.

Hayek, F. A., *Studies in Philosophy, Politics and Economics*. Routledge & Kegan Paul, London, and Chicago 1967.

Hayek, F. A. *Denationalisation of Money*. Hobart Paper Special no. 70, Institute of Economic Affairs, London 1976.

Hayek, F. A., *Law Legislation and Liberty. A new statement of the Liberal Principles of Justice and Political Economy*. Vol. I *Rules and Order*. Routledge & Kegan Paul, London 1973.

Heinemann, Klaus, *Grundzüge einer Soziologie des Geldes*. Ferdinand Enke Verlag, Stuttgart 1969. Soziologische Gegenwartsfragen. Neue Folge.

Hicks, J. R., *Critical Essays in Monetary Theory*. Clarendon Press, Oxford 1967.

Hicks, J. R., "On Capital and Growth, by L. M. Lachmann." Review article, *South African Journal of Economics*, vol. 34, no. 2, June 1966.

Hicks J. R., *A Theory of Economic History*. Oxford University Press 1969.

Hicks, J. R., *The Crisis In Keynesian Economics*. Basil Blackwell, Oxford 1974

Hicks, J. R., and Weber W., eds., *Carl Menger and the Austrian School of Economics*. Clarendon Press, Oxford 1973.

Honigsheim, Paul, "A Note on Simmel's Anthropological Interests", in K. Peter Etzkorn, *The Conflict in Modern Culture and other Essays*. Teachers College Press, New York.

Hoselitz B. and Moore, *Individuality and Society*. 1963.

Humboldt, Wilhelm von, ed., Burrow J. W., *The Limits of State Action*. Cambridge University Press 1969.

Hutchinson, T. W., *The Significance and Basic Postulates of Economic Theory*. London 1938, and New York 1960, pp. 83 ff.

Hutt, W. H., *Politically Impossible*. Hobart Paperback, The Institute of Economic Affairs, London 1971.

Hutt, W. H., *Keynesianism Retrospect and Prospect*. Henry Regnery Co., Chicago 1963.

Hyde, H. Montgomery, *John Law. A Biography*. W. H. Allen 1948.

Johnson, Elizabeth, "John Maynard Keynes: Scientist or Politician", *Journal of Political Economy* 1974.

Johnson, Harry G., *Further Essays in Monetary Economics*. Cambridge, Mass. 1972.

Johnson, Harry G., *Inflation and the Monetarist Controversy*. De Vries Lectures, North-Holland Publishing Co., Amsterdam 1972.

Johnson, Harry G., "Is there an Optimal Money Supply?", *Journal of Finance,* vol. 25, May 1970.

Kapp, K. W., "National Economy and Rational Humanism", *Kyklos*, vol. 21, 1968 p. 1.

Kehl, P., "Materielles oder ideeles Geld", *Finanzarchiv*, vol. 13, 1951/52.

Kehl, P., "Das Geld als Anspruch auf Leistungen der Gemeinschaft", in *Schmollers Jahrbuch*, vol. 72, 1952.

Kenen, Peter B., "The Costs and Benefits of the Dollar as a Reserve Currency", *Papers and Proceedings American Economic Review*, May 1973.

Keynes, John Maynard, "The General Theory of Employment", *The Quarterly Journal of Economics*, February 1937.

Keynes, John Maynard, *The Collected Writings*. vols. I–XV, Macmillan, St. Martin's Press for the Royal Economic Society 1971.

Kindleberger, Charles P., *The Formation of Financial Centers: A Study in Comparative Economic History*. Princeton Studies in International Finance, no. 36. International Finance Section Dept. of Economics Princeton University 1974.

King, Preston and Parekh B. C., eds., *Politics and Experience: Essays Presented to Professor Michael Oakeshott on the Occasion of His Retirement*. Cambridge University Press 1968.

Kittrell, Edward R., "Laissez-faire in English Classical Economics", *Journal of History of Ideas*, vol. 27, 1966.

Knapp, G. F. and Bendixen F., *Zur Staatlichen Theorie des Geldes*, ed. K. Singer, Basel and Tübingen 1958.

Knapp, G. F., *Die Staatliche Theorie Des Geldes*. 3rd Edition, Munich & Leipzig 1921. An Abridged English Edition by H. M. Lucas and J. Bonar, *The State Theory of Money*, London 1924.

Knight, F. H., "Laissez-faire Pro and Con", *Journal of Political Economy*, December 1967.

König, René, "Gestaltungsprobleme der Massengesellschaft", *Wirtschaft Gesellschaft und Kultur. Festgabe für Alfred Müller-Armack*, ed., Franz Greiss and Fritz W. Meyer.

Kuhn, Helmut, *Das Sein und das Gute*. Münich 1962.

Kuhn, Helmut, "Das Problem Der Ordnung", from *Verhandlungen des 6tn Deutschen Kongresses Für Philosophie*. Meisenheim a Glau, 1961, pp. 11–25.

Kuhn, Thomas S., *The Structure of Scientific Revolutions*. The University of Chicago Press, Chicago and London 1962.

Lachmann, L. M., "J. Hicks on Capital and Growth", review article *South African Journal of Economics*, vol. 34, no. 2, June 1966.

Lachmann, L. M., *The Legacy of Max Weber Three Essays*. Heinemann, London 1970.

Laslett, Peter, ed., *Philosophy, Politics and Society*. First Series, Basil Blackwell, Oxford, 1967.

Laslett, Peter and Runciman W. G., eds., *Philosophy, Politics and Society*. Third Series, Basil Blackwell, Oxford 1969.

Laum, B., *Heiliges Geld*. Tübingen 1924.

Laum, B., *Über das Wesen des Munzgeldes*. Halle 1929.

146   Bibliography

Laum, B., "Über die soziale Funktion der Münze", *Finanzarchiv*, vol. 13, 1951–2.

Leijohnhufvud, Axel, *Keynes and the Classics*. The Institute of Economic Affairs, London 1969.

Leijohnhufvud, Axel, *On Keynesian Economics and the Economics of Keynes. A Study of Monetary Theory*. Oxford University Press 1968.

Lekachman, Robert, ed., *Keynes' General Theory. Reports of Three Decades*. Macmillan & Co. Ltd., London 1964.

Levine, Donald N., *Simmel & Parsons: Two Approaches to the Study of Society*. The University of Chicago Press 1957.

Levine, Donald L., *Georg Simmel on Individuality and Social Forms*. Selected Writings edited and with an Introduction by D. N. Levine, The University of Chicago Press, Chicago, and London 1971.

Liebeschütz, Hans, *Von Georg Simmel zu Franz Rosenzweig*. J. C. B. Mohr, Tübingen 1970.

Lipman, Matthew, "Some Aspects of Simmel's Conception of the Individual" in *Georg Simmel 1858–1918*, ed. Kurt H. Wolff, Ohio State University Press 1959.

Locke, John, *Two Treatises of Government. A Critical Edition*. With an Introduction and Apparatus Criticus by Peter Laslett. Cambridge University Press 1960.

Löwenthal, Richard, "Unreason and Revolution", *Encounter,* vol. XXXIII, November 1969, pp. 22–34.

Löwith, Karl, *Max Weber und Karl Marx*. Archiv Für Sozialwissenschaft und Sozialpolitik, vol. 67, 1971.

Luhmann, Niklas, *Vertrauen ein Mechanismus der Reduktion sozialer Komplexität*. Ferdinand Enke Verlag, Stuttgart 1968.

Luhmann, Niklas, *Zweckbegriff und Systemrationalität*. J. C. B. Mohr (Paul Siebeck), Tübingen 1968.

Luhmann, Niklas, *Soziologische Aüfklärung. Aufsätze zur Theorie sozialer Systeme*. Westdeutscher Verlag, Köln and Obladen 1972.

Macleod, H. D., *The Theory and Practice of Banking*. London 1855.

Macleod, H. D., *The Principles of Economical Philosophy*, vol. 1, 1872.

Mann F. A., *The Legal Aspect of Money with special reference to*

Comparative Private and Public International Law. Clarendon Press, Oxford 1971.

Marget, A. W., *The Theory of Prices*. Prentice-Hall, New York, vol. I 1938, vol. II 1942.

Marschak, J., "Money Illusion and Demand Analysis", *The Review of Economic Statistics*, vol. XXV, p. 40.

Marx, Karl, *Capital*. Everyman Edn. 1930.

Marx, Karl, ed. T. B. Bottomore, *Early Writings*. London 1963.

Marx, Karl, *Marx Grundrisse*. Selected and Translated by D. McLellan. London 1971.

Marx, Karl, *Selected Essays*. Translated by H. J. Stenning, Leonard Parsons, London.

Machlup, Friz, "Euro-Dollar Creation: A Mystery Story", *Banco Nazionale Del Lavoro Quarterly Review*, 94, 1970.

McKeen, Richard, "Philosophy and Method", *Journal of Philosophy*, October 1951.

Meigs, A. James, *Money Matters*. Harper & Row Inc, New York.

Melden, A. I., "On Promising", *Mind*, vol. 65, New Series, January 1956.

Melden A. I., ed., *Essays in Moral Philosophy*. University of Washington Press, Seattle, and London 1958.

Melden A. I., *Rights and Right Conduct*. Oxford 1959.

Menger, Carl, "Problems of Economics and Sociology", *Untersuchungen über die Methode der Sozialwissenschaften und der Politischen Oekonomie Insbesondere*. Leipzig 1883. Edited and with an Introduction by Louis Schneider. Translated by Francis J. Nock. University of Illinois Press, Urbana 1963.

Menger, Carl, *Carl Menger and the Austrian School of Economics*, eds. J. R. Hicks and W. Weber. Clarendon Press, Oxford 1973.

Menger, Carl, *The Collected Works of Carl Menger*. London School of Economics and Political Science Reprints, London 1933–6.

Menger, Carl, *Principles of Economics*. Translated and edited by James Dingwall and Bert F. Hoselitz. The Free Press, Glencoe, Illinois 1950.

Meszaros, I., *Marx's Theory of Alienation*. The Merlin Press, London 1970.

Mill, John Stuart, *Principles of Political Economy with some of their Applications to Social Philosophy*. Edited with an Introduction by Sir W. J. Ashley, Longmans 1921.

Miller, C., *Studien zur Geschichte der Geldlehre*. Stuttgart and Berlin 1925.

Mises, Ludwig von, *Theory and History*. Jonathan Cape, London 1958, Yale University Press, New Haven Conn. U.S.A. 1957.

Mises, Ludwig von, *The Ultimate Foundation of Economic Science, an Essay on Method*. D. Van Nostrand Company Inc, Princeton, New Jersey 1962.

Mises, Ludwig von, *The Theory of Money and Credit (1912)*. New edition, Jonathan Cape, London 1952.

Mises, Ludwig von, *Theorie des Geldes und der Umlaufmittel*. München/Leipzig 1912.

Mitchell, Wesley C., *The Backward Art of Spending Money*. Augustus M. Kelley Inc, New York 1950.

Moggridge, D. E., *The Return to Gold. 1925: The Formulation of Economic Policy and its Critics*. Cambridge University Press. London 1969.

Murad, Anatol, *The Paradox of a Metal Standard. A Case History of Silver*. Washington 1939.

Nagel, Thomas, *The Possibility of Altruism*. Clarendon Press, Oxford 1970.

Nutter, G. Warren, *Freedom in a Revolutionary Economy* in *The American Revolution: Three Views*. American Brands Inc, New York 1975.

Nyblen, Goran, *The Problem of Summation in Economic Science. A Methodological Study with Applications to Interest Money and Cycles*. C. W. K. Gleerup, Lund 1951.

Oakeshott, Michael, *On Human Conduct*. Clarendon Press, Oxford 1975.

Oppenheimer, Peter, "The Case for Raising the Price of Gold", *Journal of Money, Credit and Banking*, vol. 1, 1969.

Ostwald, H., *Sittengeschichte der Inflation*. Berlin 1931.

Palyi, M., *The Twilight of Gold 1914–1936. Myths and Realities*. Henry Regnery Company, Chicago 1972.

Palyi, M., *Der Streit um die staatliche Theorie des Geldes*. München/Leipzig 1922.

Parkin, Charles, *The Moral Basis of Burke's Political Thought*. Cambridge University Press 1956.

Parsons, Talcott, *Economics and Society*. 1956.

Parsons, Talcott, *Theories of Society*. 1961.

Parsons, Talcott, *Social Theory and Modern Sociology*. 1967.

Paton, H. J., *The Moral Law or Kant's Groundwork of the Metaphysic of Morals*. Third Edition, Hutchinson, London 1956.

Peters, R. S., *The Concept of Motivation. Studies in Philosophical Psychology*. Edited by R. F. Holland, Second Edition, Lowe & Brydone 1960

Plamenatz, John, *Karl Marx's Philosophy of Man*. Clarendon Press, Oxford 1975.

Preiser, E., "Economic Growth. Fetish or Necessity". *Zeitschrift für die Gesammte Staatswissenschaft*, 1967.

Pearson, Gail, "The Role of Money in Economic Growth", *Quarterly Journal of Economics*, vol. 86, 1972.

Pearson, Gail, *Principal Financial Assets in the U.S.* Discussion Paper Series, no. 187, April 1971, Harvard Institute of Economic Research.

Phillips, Helen, *J. M. Keynes – Vision and Technique*. Stanford Honors Essays in Humanities, no. 1 Stanford University Press, 1952.

Popper, Karl R., *The Poverty of Historicism*. Routledge & Kegan Paul, London 1957.

Popper, Karl R., *Objective Knowledge: An Evolutionary Approach*. Clarendon Press, Oxford 1972.

Pribram, Karl, *Die Entstehung der individualistischen Sozialphilosophie*. Leipzig 1912.

Pribram, Karl, *Conflicting Patterns of Thought*. Washington D.C. 1949.

Rankin, Bayard, "The History of Probability and the Changing Concept of the Individual", *Journal of the History of Ideas*, vol. 27, 1966.

Rawls, John, "Justice as Fairness", *Philosophical Review*, 1958. Reprinted in *Philosophy, Politics and Society*, Second Series, eds. Peter Laslett and W. G. Runciman. Blackwell, Oxford 1969.

Rawls, John, *A Theory of Justice*. Clarendon Press, Oxford 1971.

Riesterer, Berthold P., *Karl Löwith's View of History. A Critical Appraisal of Historicism*. Martinus Nijhoff, The Hague.

Rist, Charles, *History of Monetary and Credit Theory from John Law to the Present Day*. George Allen & Unwin, London 1940.

Rist, Charles, *The Triumph of Gold*. Philosophical Library Inc., New York 1961.

Roberts, Paul Craig, *Alienation and the Soviet Economy*. University of New Mexico Press, Albuquerque.

Roberts, Paul Craig and Stephenson, Matthew A., *Marx's Theory of Exchange Alienation and Crisis*. Hoover Institution Press, Stanford University 1973.

Robinson, Joan, *Collected Economic Papers*. Basil Blackwell, Oxford 1965.

Rueff, Jacques, *The Monetary Sin of the West*. Translation of *Le Péché Monétaire de l'Occident*. Librairie Plon 1971, Macmillan, New York 1972.

Rueff, Jacques, *Balance of Payments*. Proposals for the resolution of the most pressing world problem of our time. Macmillan, New York 1967.

Rueff, Jacques and Hirsch, Fred, *The Role and the Rule of Gold: an Argument*. International Finance Section, Princeton University 1965.

Russell, Henry B., *International Monetary Conferences: Their Purpose, Character and Results*. Harper Bros, London and New York 1898.

Ryle, Gilbert, *Dilemmas*. The Tarner Lectures 1953. Cambridge University Press 1954.

Ryle, Gilbert, *The Concept of Mind*. Hutchinson's University Library, London 1949.

Salz, Arthur, "Die irrationale Grundlage der Kapitalistischen Wirtschaft und Gesellschafts Ordnung". In *Soziologische Studien Alfred Weber gewidmet*. Heidelberg 1930.

Sayers, R. S., *Central Banking after Bagehot*. Oxford University Press 1957.

Schmölders, Günter, Schroder, R. and Seidenfus H. St., *J M Keynes Als Psychologe*. Duncker and Humblot, Berlin 1956.

Schmölders, Günter, *Von der Quantitätstheorie zur Liquiditätstheorie des Geldes*. Abhandlungen der Geistes und Sozialwissenschaftlichen Klasse. Jahrgang 1960, Nr. 12, Franz Steiner, Wiesbaden 1961.

Schmölders, Günter, "J. M. Keynes's Beitrag zur Ökonomischen Verhaltensforschung", in G. Schmölders, R. Schröder, H. St. Seidenfus, *John Maynard Keynes als Psychologe*. Berlin 1956.

Schmölders, G., Ökonomische Verhaltungsforschung. ORDO 5, Bd Düsseldorf München.

Schmölders, G., *Psychologie des Geldes*. Reinbach 1966.

Schmoller, G., "Simmel's Philosophie Des Geldes", *Schmoller's Jahrbücher*, 1901, no. 3.

Schoeck, Helmut, *Envy: A Theory of Social Behaviour*. Secker & Warburg, London 1969.

Schumpeter, Joseph A., *Das Wesen Des Geldes*. Edited from MS and with an Introduction by Fritz Karl Mann, Vandenhoeck & Ruprecht, Göttingen 1970.

Schumpeter, Joseph A., *History of Economic Analysis*. Oxford University Press, New York and George Allen & Unwin, London 1954.

Shackle G. L. S., "Keynes and Today's Establishment in Economic Theory: A View", *Journal of Economic Literature*, June 1973, vol. XI, no. 2.

Silberner, Edmund, *Moses Hess. Geschichte seines Lebens*. E. J. Brill, Leiden 1966.

Simmel, Georg, *Die Philosophie Des Geldes*. Second Edition, Duncker und Humblot, Leipzig 1907.

Simmel, Georg, *Hauptprobleme der Philosophie*. G. J. Goschen'sche Verlagshandlung 1910.

Simmel, Georg, "Soziologische Vorlesungen", Gehalten an der Universität Berlin 1899. Reprinted: Society for Social Research, University of Chicago, 1931, Series 1, no. 11.

Simmel, Georg, *Soziologische Untersuchungen über die Formen der Vergesellschaftung*. Duncker und Humblot, Berlin 1958.

Simmel, Georg, *The Conflict in Modern Culture and Other Essays*. Translated with an introduction by K. Peter Etzkorn. Teachers College Press, Columbia University, New York.

Simmel, Georg, ed., Weingartner, R. H., *Experience and Culture* 1962.

Simon, H. A., "Theories of Decision Making in Economics and Behavioral Science", *American Economic Review*, June 1959, vol. 49.

Simons, Henry, "Rules versus Authorities in Monetary Policy", *Journal of Political Economy*, vol. 44, 1936. Reprinted in *American Economic Association Readings in Monetary Theory*, vol. V, p. 363.

Simons, Henry, *Economic Policy for a Free Society*. University of Chicago Press 1951.

Smithies, Arthur, "Keynes Revisited", *Quarterly Journal of Economics*, August 1972, vol. LXXXVI.

Spykman, Nicholas, J., *The Social Theory of Georg Simmel*. Chicago University Press, Chicago 1925.

St. John Stevas, Norman, *Walter Bagehot*. London 1963.

Stigler, George, "The Economics of Carl Menger", *Journal of Political Economy,* vol. 45, April 1937.

Stigler, George, "The Economics of Information", *Journal of Political Economy*, June 1961, vol. 69, pp. 213–25.

Streissler, Erich W., "Menger's Theories of Money and Uncertainty. A Modern Interpretation" in J. R. Hicks and W. Weber, ed., *Carl Menger and the Austrian School of Economics*. Clarendon Press, Oxford 1973.

Susman, M. von Bewdemann, *Die Geistige Gestalt Georg Simmels*. 1959.

Sweezy, Paul M., "Keynes the Economist" in *The New Economics: Keynes's Influence on Theory and Public Policy*, ed. Seymour E. Harris. Dobson, London 1960.

Taylor, Charles, *Hegel*. Cambridge University Press 1975.

Thomas, Lewis, "Language and Human Communication", *Dialogue*, vol. 8, 1975, no. 3/4, pp. 30–1, Washington D.C.

Townshend, Hugh, "Liquidity-Premium and the Theory of Value". *The Economic Journal*, March 1937, vol. XLVII.

Trevelyan, G. M., *English Social History*. London 1942.

Unger, Erwin, *The Greenback Era; a Social and Political History of American Finance 1865–79*. Princeton University Press and Oxford University Press.

Walter, E. V., Simmel's Sociology of Power: The Architecture of Politics, in Kurt H. Wolff, ed., *Georg Simmel 1858–1918*, Ohio State University Press, Columbus, Ohio 1959.

Walters, A. A., *Money in Boom and Slump*. Hobart Paper 44, The Institute of Economic Affairs, London 1969.

Weber, Max, *The Theory of Social & Economic Organization*. London 1947. Part 1 of *Wirtschaft und Gesellschaft* translated from the German by A. R. Henderson and Talcott Parsons with an Introduction by Talcott Parsons.

Weingartner, Rudolph H., "Form and Content in Simmel's Philosophy of Life" from *Georg Simmel. The Conflict in Modern Culture and other Essays*. Translated, with an Introduction, by K. Peter Etzkorn, 1968.

Weingartner, Rudolph H., *Experience and Culture*. Wesleyan University Press, 1962, p. 84.

Wolff, Kurt H., *The Sociology of Georg Simmel*. The Free Press of Glencoe, Illinois 1950.

Wolff, Kurt H., ed., *Georg Simmel 1858–1918. A Collection of Essays*. Ohio State University Press, Columbia, Ohio 1959.

Wolodin, W. S., *Keynes: eine Ideologie des Monopolkapitals*. Berlin 1955

Wrong, Dennis, ed., *Makers of Modern Social Science: Max Weber*. Prentice-Hall, Inc., Englewood Cliffs, N.J. 1970.

Yeager, Leyland B., "Economics and Principles", *Southern Economic Journal* April 1976, vol. 42, no. 4.

Yeager, Leyland B., *The International Money Mechanism*. Holt Rinehart and Winston, New York 1968.

Yeager, Leyland B., *International Monetary Relations: Theory History and Policy*. Harper & Row, New York 1966.

Index

With some exceptions this Index includes only books and articles referred to in the main text. All others will be found in the Bibliography and Appendix.